Studies in Penderecki

Prestige Publications, Inc.
Princeton, New Jersey

EDITOR
Ray Robinson

CO–EDITOR
Regina Chłopicka

TECHNICAL EDITOR
Darryl Miller

TECHNICAL ASSISTANCE
Robyn Howland

COVER DESIGN
Ruth Robinson

PROOF READING
Grażyna Zakrzewska

EDITORIAL BOARD
Regina Chłopicka,
Cracow, Poland

Irina Nikolska
Moscow, Russia

Paul Patterson
London, England

Ray Robinson
West Palm Beach, Florida

Wolfram Schwinger
Stuttgart, Germany

Robert Shankovich
Pittsburgh, Pennsylvania

Marek Stachowski
Cracow, Poland

Mieczysław Tomaszewski
Cracow, Poland

Allen Winold
Bloomington, Indiana

CORRESPONDING BOARD
Allmuth Behrendt
Leipzig, Germany

Krzysztof Droba
Cracow, Poland

Rûta Goštautienė
Vilnius, Lithuania

Wes Janzen
Langley, British Columbia

Cindy Karen McTee
Denton, Texas

©1998 Prestige Publications, Inc.

ISBN 0–911009–10–8

ISSN 1097–5977

Studies in Penderecki

Prestige Publications, Inc. Volume I, 1998

REVIEWS OF BOOKS

RESEARCH REPORT

CONTRIBUTORS

GUIDELINES FOR PUBLICATIONS

LIST OF PENDERECKI'S WORKS

ACKNOWLEDGMENTS

The Editorial Board wishes to express its appreciation to those contributors whose generosity has made this publication possible: Ned and Lucy Fox, Mitchell and Zofia Kafarski, Yaga Olszewski, the Cracow Academy of Music, and Palm Beach Atlantic College.

Editor's Column

Krzysztof Penderecki (b. 1933) stands at the apex of a career that has extended beyond four decades and has attracted the attention of the musical connoisseur and the general public in most countries of the world. Initially recognized as the leader of a potent and creative avant–garde movement in Poland in the early–1960's, Penderecki has gone on to establish himself as one of the most important composers and conductors in the world today. His compositions are now performed regularly on symphonic programs and in the opera houses of Europe and America, and he has acquired the reputation of being one of the most original creators of his generation. On the North American continent alone, he has received twelve commissions which have resulted in an equal number of first performances.

Less known is the attention Penderecki has attracted from scholars and writers. More than thirty doctoral dissertations have been produced world–wide and approximately 1000 articles on the composer and his music have appeared in periodicals and newspapers around the world. It is clear that there is a significant international interest in his life and works. It is doubtful if any other composer in the history of music has received such recognition and scrutiny during his lifetime.

In recognition of his contributions to the music of our time, a group of scholars came together in Poland on the occasion of Penderecki's 60th birthday celebration in 1993 to discuss how this burgeoning interest in Penderecki scholarship could be enhanced, focused and made available to the world–wide academic and musical community. These initial discussions led to a meeting in June 1994 in the Polish city of Cracow where a mission statement was developed, an editorial board was identified and elected, and a decision was made to move forward with a plan to create an annual publication with the working title "Studies in Penderecki". It was also decided that the language of the journal would be English. The present volume is a result of these efforts.

The Editorial Board has chosen to focus this initial volume on a retrospective view of the composer's career by commissioning four major articles on the topic: "Krzysztof Penderecki: A career in retrospect". The authors of these lead articles have all studied about and written extensively on the composer's music, but they represent different points of view from the standpoint of their background and geographical orientation. Consequently, these essays present four contrasting views of the composer's stylistic evolution. Supporting these four lead articles are analyses of two of the composer's most recent works, reviews of performances in various countries, and reviews of two of the latest studies on Penderecki and his music. Of special interest in this first issue, and what will be a regular feature of these volumes, is the research report, which in this issue focuses on Penderecki research in America universities.

Subsequent volumes will deal with topics such as "Penderecki and the avant–garde" (1999) and "Penderecki and the theater" (2000). The contents of each issue will include work analyses; reviews of performances, books and major articles; and a research report on a phase of the composer's work that is consistent with the general topic of the issue. An outline of "General Guidelines for Annual Publications" is included at the end of this volume to give the reader insight into the long range planning process of the Editorial Board

It is the desire of the Editorial Board that *Studies in Penderecki* will contribute to a broader understanding of the life and work of one of the 20th century's major musical personalities and thereby contribute to continuing research in the history of 20th century music. Your comments about this volume are welcome.

Ray Robinson
West Palm Beach, Florida
January, 1998

Krzysztof Penderecki
CRACOW

"My Iliad and Odyssey"

> I am concerned with only one thing: getting closer, slowly, in a roundabout way, walking back and forth, walking away and then coming back, but always with a clear goal in mind. Closer to what? To knowledge, although I don't know what knowledge, to a conclusion, to understanding,

writes Czesław Miłosz in his volume *The Unknown Land*, expressing the general condition of humanity, in particular artists, at the close of the century. We are in a labyrinth—we enter in many ways, exit and return with a very vague idea of our goal. We want to assess, understand—not only our own existence, but also the closing century. I am afraid, however, that this is impossible at this moment.

Italo Calvino in one of his "American Lectures" expressed this inability most forcibly:

> Sometimes I have the feeling that some epidemic has overcome humanity and struck its most characteristic feature, that is, speech: a kind of a linguistic plague, which manifests itself in the loss of cognitive power and openness, in a tendency for automatic restriction of means of expression to the most general, anonymous and abstract formulations, to the blurring of meaning, to the blunting of the shaft of expression, to extinguishing every spark produced when words clash with a new context.

This feeling of discord of language with reality was already expressed by our *fin de siècle* predecessors. But we are in an even worse situation. A hundred years ago art had an individualistic character; today we are overpowered by a blurred, mass culture. In the same essay on "Accuracy," Calvino wrote:

> We are immersed in an unbroken flow of images; the ubiquitous mass media keep on transforming the world into images and reproducing it through a phantasmagoria of mirror tricks.... A large part of this cloud of pictures fades abruptly like a dream that leaves no traces in the memory. But the feeling of alienation and unpleasantness remains.

The dictate of the mass media reduces everything into a pulp. Homogenized culture doesn't distinguish levels, destroys hierarchies, puts high and low culture on the same footing. In pursuit of commercial success, managers provide intellectual nourishment in increasingly more attractive wrappings and arrangements: famous tenors sing popular arias in unison at sports events; technically sophisticated products—video cassettes and compact discs—are a substitute for live contact with literature, film, theater, music. In this kaleidoscope of information, what suffers most is the imagination. The crisis of the imagination is our greatest problem.

An instinctive reaction is to escape, to withdraw into one's own world; but will this protect our creative powers? In Lusławice I surrounded my estate and my garden with a high wall, in the belief that—in line with symbolic thinking—this wall would strengthen the inner powers that grew there. Such a *hortus conclusus* is a world in itself, my cosmos, whose harmony I shape myself. As I lay out trees in a row and put down lawns and flower beds, I am aware of building my own Arcadia, and I am also certain—as my many predecessors—that I am surrendering myself to "the most natural, charming and virtuous of all arts." Acting in accordance with earlier traditions, in my garden I have also laid out a labyrinth. Here I feel confident, I know the way in and out, I have built it following the principles of *construzione legittima.*

It's a different matter with the labyrinth of creation and of the world. How can we achieve an artistic goal in the entanglement of existence, in this chaos we are living in?

It is comforting to realize that the labyrinth—a metaphor for life—always contains irrational as well as unpredictable and predictable elements that we can take control of. The way to fulfillment is only through wandering around aimlessly. *Nur der Umweg führt zur Vollkommenheit*—suggests Gustav René Hocke, the author of the classic work *Die Welt als Labyrinth*. Surveying the entire 20th century, I have come to realize that this intricate structure is the destiny of the artist. Stravinsky, Schönberg, Picasso, Witkacy, Kantor. The last mentioned wrote openly:

> If development is conventionally shown as a straight line, as a spiral, or as concentric lines, then my output would be graphically represented as a labyrinth. The lack of an exit shows that we are progressing well. In art—of course.

Therefore we have to look for hope in paradoxes. The condition of art now really is at a dead end. In all fields of creation we observe the exhaustion of ideas and of material, and in music the over–exploitation of the possibilities. In my *Threnody* of 1960, the string instruments sound like percussion instruments. Today there are no such creative innovations. Despite the fact that we can draw from so many sources of inspiration, the language of art has become trite and impoverished. We have found ourselves at a point where the most creative act is to open the door behind ourselves. How far we are from the artists of the first avant–garde who had—although this also turned out to be a Utopia—a clear–cut goal before them. We are more like those Baudelairean travellers who start on a journey just for the sake of starting.

But I don't want to fall into typical *fin de siècle* pessimism. Therefore I reject the beautiful image from the last volume of *Facing the River* by Miłosz:

> The gate of the Black Garden closes, peace, peace, what is finished, is finished.

I believe neither in the post–modernist "author's death," nor in the "decline of the great form." I reject the present fashionable blurring and disintegration of the structure of a work. I refuse to accept the victory of sophistry over imagination. It is necessary to have a keen intelligence and consciousness, but also to listen intently to one's inner world. As an Israeli writer, Amos Oz, accurately expressed it:

> When a man sits down to, say, compose, on the one hand he must be alert and have senses as keen as an assassin on the Night of the Long Knives, when every moment may be critical, and on the other—he must lose himself as if in sleep. If he is only alert, he will not create a work. If he loses himself completely in sleep, music will not be created either.

It is necessary to be true to one's self. This period of stagnation and obliteration of the individual from art cannot last forever. Art must be restored to life. I am not a prophet, I can't prophesy what paintings painters will paint or how music will sound in the future. But I believe in the future avant–garde, not as an institution (it is common knowledge that it is institutionalization that has damaged the avant–garde movement this century) but as the essence of true creation.

"And who will hold the vanguard before me," asks Charlemagne in the *Song of Roland*. This question about the vanguard and the avant–garde is still relevant today.

Mieczysław Tomaszewski

CRACOW

Penderecki's Dialogs and Games With Time and Place on the Earth

The Roots and 'Time Before Time'

> I am very far from mythologizing my home town, although recently (the statement dates back to 1992) this has been so popular. The pre–war Dębica could prove a suitable material for that. A spirit of Emperor Francis Joseph hovered over this little Galician town; I remember the *Gemütlichkeit* atmosphere typical of little towns: in my family home, for example, we played music every Sunday.[1]

Penderecki would not have been himself if he had not added: "But this does not explain anything after all."

It does seem to explain something, it sheds some light, it gives one something to think about. The town, founded in the 14th century, thus rich in tradition, became "Galician" at the end of the 18th century;[2] in the mid–19th century, when the Cracow–Lvov railroad was constructed, it received a connection with the outside world; in the 20th century it stood out as a capital of the surrounding district. It used to be inhabited by Poles and Jews, who lived there together and perhaps side by side too, supervised by Austrian officials, who were often strongly influenced by Polish language and culture. Krzysztof Penderecki's father, attorney by profession, was the son of an Austrian official, while on the distaff side he came from an Armenian family. The composer's mother was of German origin: her grandfather had arrived there as a forester; Penderecki's father ran the bank of Dębica and headed the local branch of the "Sokół" organization,[3] which stood guard over the patriotic traditions of the town. The religious traditions were assumed by the mother. The father had a mild inclination towards socialism, while in his spare time he used to play music in the company of his friends. There was a time when through the open garden window the prayers and dance tunes of the Chassidim could be heard from the local synagogue, whereas later the family heard how the Nazi extermination policies were implemented. The child's memory also noted the picture, seen through the front window, of the market square where the underground Polish Army "bandits" were being hanged.

As a boy Penderecki diligently read *Little Lord Fauntleroy* and *The Heart* by Amicis, then Stevenson's *Treasure Island* and the books on American Indians by Cooper, Curwood and May. A few years later, when he approached his final examinations at school, he was absorbed by Homer, Hesiod, Euripides and Virgil, and everything that had to do with ancient Greek and Roman culture. The grand world, remote both in time and space, was a strong draw. He recollects his desire to become a sailor, then, right afterwards, a village surgeon, and then, when his choices became more mature, a painter, architect or art historian, and finally a violinist. He takes lessons from rather haphazardly chosen local teachers, he joins a band which plays at dancing parties and weddings, with a group of classmates he also plays at official school occasions. Among his first compositions is a violin concerto, written according to the principles he learned studying the scores of other composers.

His arrival in Cracow in 1951 opened new perspectives: it both broadened and deepened his personality, it let in new experiences and made his self–realization possible. Excellent teachers tutored him privately, he completed Cracow's music high school within two years[4] (it was the school's top period), and the road was open for him to go to college. Common sense led him to abandoning the career of a violin virtuoso and focusing on the theory of music. Fascination with counterpoint guided him towards composition, which he gradually discovered as the principal goal of his professional activity and existence. Franciszek Skołyszewski, the master always so fondly remembered by Penderecki, awakened his imagination and ignited his passionate interest, showing him the essence and possibilities of this age–old technique, whereas Professor Artur Malawski tried to force his pupil to adhere to its canons. "I never agreed with him"[5], Penderecki will say years later. It so happened that *Epitaphium Artur Malawski in memoriam* (unpublished) for violin and kettledrums was Penderecki's graduation work in June 1958.

This is the time of enchantment with contemporary music, which in this part of the world was then being let out of forced seclusion only slowly and gradually. Bartók and Stravinsky dominate in Penderecki's world, but apart from *The Miraculous Mandarin* and *The Rite of Spring,* there is room there for the works such as Honegger's *Joan of Arc at the Stake* or Orff's *Carmina Burana,* which he is now able to get to know not only from the radio but also sometimes from the repertoire of Cracow Philharmonic. What follows is his acquisition or rejection of the novelties which keep creeping in from behind the Iron Curtain, such as the twelve–tone, serial and aleatory techniques. Apart from that, the composer absorbs the literature which attracts and moves, notably Dostoyevsky and Tolstoy, *Dziady* and *Chłopi,*[6] and all the three *Comedies*: the

Divine, the *Un–Divine*[7] and the *Human.*[8]

The encounter with the opportunities which the environment of Cracow offered to a high school graduate from Dębica did not awaken a composer in him right away. He was quite as likely to become a classical scholar or art historian.

> When I studied music in Cracow, I spent almost an equal amount of time studying classical languages and philosophy. I attended the university lectures given by Tadeusz Sinko and Roman Ingarden.[9]

And he concludes:

> In old Cracow I could feel what the continuity and unity of tradition meant; I saw myself as brought up in the Mediterranean culture.[10]

One might add, not without a tone of malicious irony: it was the time of the greatest triumphs of socialist realism in the culture of the Soviet block.

The set of themes and ideas which Penderecki draws on in his work, a repertoire of obsessions and archetypes, seems to have its root cause not only in his talent and character. The historical time and place have had their contribution here as well.

The Effective Entry, 1958–60: the Phase of *Psalms of David*

The composer's entry onto the Polish and soon enough also the European stage of contemporary music was effective indeed. The three highest awards won at one competition, a prospect of a scholarship abroad, more and more numerous performances of the awarded works, commissions to write new works offered by highly prestigious institutions and festivals,[11] publication proposals both from within and outside of Poland, an almost unanimous chorus of praise from the reviewers. Such success could have turned the heads of many people.

Penderecki is 25 years old, works as an assistant to the Head of Composition Department, Stanisław Wiechowicz, and in his portfolio he has a series of compositions in which he manifests his view of the world, life and art. In several compositions of these early years, performed in the spotlight of the critics and the public, he has roughly outlined the plan which seems to anticipate the program actually realized in his more mature years in his finest compositions. It is already here that we deal with combining water and fire, tradition and the avant–garde with reaching out to boundaries, ringing the high tone or engaging in a game, superficially deprived of any *arrière–pensées.*

Psalms of David (1958) for mixed choir and percussion were written by Penderecki to four selected passages from the *Psalter* by Jan Kochanowski.[12] The texts are highly significant, they cannot but be taken to be the author's personal confession. Psalmody mingles here with sonorism, German thinking with the twelve tone, pointillist breakup of the soft harmony of percussion with *a cappella* singing. It is one of the three works, which were awarded at the ZKP[13] Young Composers' Competition in 1959.

Emanations (1958), next of the awarded works: a constellation of harmonies, scattered according to pointillist technique, scored for two string ensembles. It constitutes the realization of a nearly devilish idea: the instruments of one of the orchestras were tuned half a tone higher: "I was lucky that I started my career at the time when there was still so much to discover."[14]

Strophes (1959) is the presentation of the composer's early ideals and skeptical questions, in which he uses the words of Meander, Isaiah, Jeremiah and Omar Khayyam, in their original versions: "How beautiful can a human be, if human he is." The respect for the natural prosody and intonation of speech goes along with elaborate serialization experienced under the influence of the scores of Boulez.

Dimensions of Time and Silence (1960), or the pure spatial–temporal play of sounds and tone colors scored for a 40–voice strong choir, percussion and strings. Penderecki split the speech into separate syllables which he made meaningless and had them spin in silence according to a very strict order.

This is what the debut was like. From today's perspective (1998) the author of *Psalms* and *Emanations* wants to assure us that "the contrast between avant–garde and tradition seemed [to him] only superficial from the very beginning. "You cannot", he says,

> tear yourself away either from the musical past in the strict sense or, even less so, from the cultural heritage in the broadest sense.[15]

These years could be called the time of entry and anticipation. It is already here that Penderecki's conceptual program places man between heaven and earth. Words have a great deal to contribute both in the area of general meanings and at the atomic level of language, while music oscillates from the meaningful to the ludic form and constitutes the combination of the post–Schoenbergian and the post–Dutch trends. In accordance with the tendency salient in the post–Webern epoch, he combines the pointillist texture of sound form with the aphoristic character.

Time of Trials and Experiments, 1960–1966: the Phase of Threnody

It is difficult not to believe Penderecki when, looking back on his life, he says:

> I have never been interested in sound and form just for their own sake, which has saved me from the avant–garde disease, the futile emptiness and boredom of abstract formal solutions.[16]

It is difficult to believe him, for the series of scores he put on the agendas of conductors and orchestras in the early sixties might throw the sincerity of this statement into doubt.

Not all conductors were then able to cope with this music, written down by means of marks rather than notes; there were orchestras which, as the composer recollects, "became furious" and refused to cooperate. Penderecki's name was perceived not only as belonging to but as being directly synonymous with the avant–garde of the time. The earlier avant–garde was created by Boulez, Nono, Berio, Stockhausen, Xenakis and Cage, each in his own vein. Penderecki began to lead the new avant–garde as a representative of its most radical trend. As Krzysztof Droba reminds us,

> the trend has been labeled sonorism and perceived as our national specialty: what was sonoristic was then regarded in the West and East as Polish.[17]

Threnody became the manifesto of the trend, and it was followed by numerous other scores, which took advantage of the exceptional success of the former.

> *Threnody* (1960) was composed for 52 string instruments, which in Penderecki's design were to play the role of percussion and wind instruments. The articulation devised by the composer, accompanied by the unique texture (clusters) and precise form produced the extraordinary, moving expression. It is generally known that originally the work was to be called *"8'36"*, which stood for the time it took to be performed. It was only the impressions of the audiences that made the composer change the title to *Threnody* and add the complementary dedication (*To the Victims of Hiroshima*).
>
> *Anáklasis* (1960) for 42 strings and 6 percussion groups was a new challenge to the musical establishment. It brought the harmonies unknown before, ruled by Penderecki's imagination and by mathematics. For some it was "a brilliant, enthralling percussion concerto"[18], for others "the sound background, and nothing else"[19].
>
> *String Quartet No. 1* (1960), handed on to the performers in a graphic shape almost without notes, exploited the catalogue of techniques familiar

already from *Threnody*. All the possible shades of soft sound patterns preceded and followed the climax, which was devoted to pure harmonies. An admirer of Haydn's, Beethoven's or Bartók's quartets could become indignant, or wonder.

Polymorphia (1961), again for strings, this time broken into 48 independent voices, and again an unconventional articulation, the counterpoint of clusters and glissandos. A moment of astonishment when reading the score: the "melody" of the violas turns out to be determined by an electrocardiographic curve. A moment of astonishment while listening to the work: the final, impossibly grating chords resolve into a pure C Major. It was from this "cathartic" chord, (i.e. from the ending) that Penderecki set out to compose the work.

Flourescences (1962), or a study of unusual, sometimes even shocking tone colors, an attempt at a translation of both action painting (tachism) and futurism into music. The composer enlarged the full orchestra forces to include a series of provoking "instruments", such as typewriter, hacksaw or an alarm siren.

De Natura Sonoris I (1966), scored for large orchestra as well, seems to be "painting" some kind of sound landscape with it or perhaps rather a "still life with instruments", although the title indicates the wish to probe into the sound matter itself, the sound *per se*.

The beginning of the 1960's allowed Penderecki to construct a unique set of techniques, an experimental laboratory, the scope of which was limited by nothing but his own imagination of harmonies and sound patterns. The "fury" of orchestras and audiences excited him even more. "I wanted to outrage them," he disclosed once, "and I managed to succeed."

These years of trials and experiments witnessed something which could be called the outburst of the elements, the liberation of instrumental sounds from the limits of convention, the rejection of numerous musical taboos. Penderecki checked out the boundaries of serial techniques, beyond which boredom sets in, and those of aleatory procedures which lead to chaos. He experienced the limits of sonorism, beyond which lies barbarity. Having demonstrated his curiosity and courage, this disciple of a wizard was able to put the elements under control and make them obey the requirements of expression. Finally, he dared to abandon the field which he regarded as futile.

As the first monographer of Penderecki, Ludwik Erhardt thus commented on this: "he slighted the laurel of an avant–garde artist, he became a creative artist. The avant–garde has never forgiven him that."[20]

The Breakthrough and the First Synthesis, 1965–1971: the Phase of The Passion.

The breakthrough had its anticipations, the successful and the unsuccessful. Back in 1962 Penderecki suddenly receives a commission from PWM publishers and decides to compose a *Stabat mater* for three choirs. In spirit it took after Ockeghem and Palestrina, which is rather surprising when put in the environment of "treatises" on the nature of sound he had been writing at the time. The work is widely known to be the beginning of the *Passion*. In 1963 he produced the *Death Brigade* [*Todes Brigade*] for the Polish Radio. The musical means were not able to match the horror of the theme: it was more proper to remain silent than to cry out. The tape was shelved, but the theme of annihilation and earthly apocalypse was to keep returning with a nearly obsessive force.

Penderecki went through the breakthrough almost naturally, as if he had turned over a new leaf, but kept reading his own text. The text suddenly became serious, the lucid element was transformed into a dramatic one, the expression labeled "pure" turned into one truly emotionally loaded, the provoking attitude became expressive. Before the first bars of *Passion* were played in Münster in March 1966, he said:

> It is enough to have some religious conviction and express it. I have nothing against treating my music as a 'confession'; in this respect, I am a Romantic.[21]

A series of grand scores, with respect to both theme and size, followed: after *the Passion*, there is *Dies Irae* and *The Devils of Loudun*, both movements of *Utrenya* and *Kosmogonia*, all as if carried by the same wave.

Passio et Mors Domini Nostri Jesu Christi secundum Lucam (1965–1966). It was a confession but a challenge too, a gauntlet flung at the imagination of critics of modern music. One would have to be blind not to be able to see a masterpiece in this work. Courageously, perhaps proudly too, the composer takes up Bach's form ("without Bach I would never have written my *Passion*"[22]) and the eternal, universal theme.

> I reached for the archetype of the Passion, to express not only the martyrdom and death of Christ, but the cruelty of our own age, the martyrdom of Auschwitz. Through the tension and dramatism of music, I wanted to draw the audience into the center of events, as was the case in medieval mystery plays, where nobody stood aside. Everybody can be drawn in by the mob, the *turba*, who demand the crucifixion of Christ, just as it is everybody that is included in the redemption.[23]

In the performance of the work what happens between Gethsemane and Golgotha happens here and now. And only musicologists and composers know how much mastery, mathematics and geometry is hidden in the score.

Dies Irae (1967), subtitled as "*oratorium ob memoriam in perniciei castris in Oświęcim necatorum in exstinguibilem reddendam,*"[24] speaks the language of an expressionistic poster. The choir speaks and sings less frequently than it shouts and whistles, the soloists reach and cross the borders of their own vocal capabilities, the orchestra includes the siren, catena (chain) and lastra—sonorism turns into *bruitism*. From the fragments of texts, which the composer took from the Bible as well as the works of Aeschylus, Valéry, Aragon, Broniewski[25] and Różewicz[26], the audience is able to recognize only the key words: what reaches them is the verbal squash, beaming with expression. The extreme character of the means of expression provoked violent reactions on the part of avant–garde defenders: Claude Rostand had not heard anything in the work which would go beyond "trashy emotionality, throwing the dust of tawdry effects into people's eyes."[27] In the interpretation of Penderecki himself, the oratorio, constructed of three grand themes: *Lamentatio, Apocalypsis* and *Apotheosis*, has been designed to illustrate the victory of life over death from the apocalyptic as well as purely human perspective. The last movement closes with the words from a poem of Paul Valéry's, *Le cimètire marin*: "The wind is rising. Let us try to live."[28]

The Devils of Loudun (1969) attacked another of the "extreme" themes, which Penderecki had been thinking about for a long time (*i.e.* "Mother Joan of Angels",[29] "Witches of Salem", and maybe also Prokofiev's *Fiery Angel* opera). What was a draw for him was the sharply delineated borderline between the spheres which normally permeate each other: the sacred and the profane, the mystical and the erotic. The hero of the opera, Father Grandier, "consciously chooses to descend to the bottom in order to run away from himself and find God"[30]. Again there are extreme effects, culminating in the *auto da fé* which is a reference, perhaps subconsciously made, to *Joan of Arc at the Stake*. "When I wrote my first opera, nobody was interested in the [contemporary] opera"[31]. His attempt to tackle the abandoned genre was taken to be another *faux pas*. And *The Devils of Loudun* gradually entered the stages of all the more courageous opera theaters in the world.

Utrenya I (*The Entombment of Christ* 1970) and II (*The Resurrection* 1971) allowed Penderecki to test himself on a new ground: the sacred music tradition of the Eastern Orthodox Church. Fascinated with the climate and high dramatism of Orthodox liturgy, with which he became familiar during his travels, he yielded to the temptation to create its reflection, its sound photograph. Listening to *Utrenya* with eyes closed, both to its ecstatic and contemplative parts, both the chants cited and the ones composed "in the style and spirit," one might have the feeling of participating in the rite itself. After Musorgsky's *Boris Godunov*, Janácek's *Glagolitic Mass*, and Szymanowski's first act of *King Roger*, European culture has been enriched with a new shade of understanding and feeling Orthodoxy.

Thus within the period of just a few years the "new Penderecki" came into being. Not everybody was able to reconcile him with the author of *Polymorphia* or *Fluorescences*. But as a matter of fact, none of the harmonies discovered by him in the early days turned out to be fruitless: they only started to serve a purpose now. They made it possible for the themes of evil and darkness, injustice and intolerance, annihilation and hope to be presented musically, which means that they also made it possible for the world of sound (already in the form of music) to be written into culture.

It might be worthwhile to remember that in those years in this part of Europe nobody dared to or felt the need to take up themes and genres of sacred music, except Penderecki. He did this with the purposefulness of a mature artist. "My art," he said remembering those days,

> stems from profoundly Christian roots and aims at reconstructing a human metaphysical universe shattered by the cataclysms of the 20th century. The restoration of the sacred dimension of reality is the only way to save humanity. Art should be the source of difficult hope.[32]

The Intermediary Period: Years of Sublimation, 1971–1975—Phase of Magnificat

Almost imperceptibly a new tone starts ringing in Penderecki's music, a new form and a new sound quality slowly reach maturity. After the years of highest tension in expression, sometimes glaring, sometimes bordering on the hysterical, a calmer period sets in. Penderecki puts mutes on the emotions, chooses themes which have cast off their weight, gloominess or dramatic breach, revives the purely instrumental music, and tends to prefer gentler harmonies, and textures closer to the fabric rather than distinct strokes. On the instrumental side the period brings along *Partita* (1972), Concerto No. 1 for Violoncello (1972), *Symphony No. 1* (1973) and *The Awakening of Jacob* (1974), and on the vocal or vocal–instrumental side, *Ecloga VIII* (1972), *Canticum canticorum* (1973) and *Magnificat* (1974).

Ecloga VIII (1972) is scored for six male voices of the famous British King's Singers. One may see in it a virtuoso study for 18 types of vocal articulation from breathing in and whisper to falsetto and laughter. But in fact in front of our eyes a scene of love incantations is evoked, directly taken out of Virgil's bucolic idylls. Only a masterful performance can turn the *le petit rien* into the work shimmering with multiple shades of emotions expressed in varying harmonies.

Canticum canticorum Salomonis (1973) brings an attempt to tackle one of the most beautiful texts in the history of the world, dealing with both the human and transcendental love. Nowhere before has Penderecki's music sounded equally refined. Nowhere before has it been produced by such subtle twists of counterpoint either. Barbara Cisowska thus ends her analytical essay on *Song of Songs*: "*Canticum canticorum* brings the message of love which is the expression of the affirmation of existence. Penderecki's music announces the return to traditional categories of beauty."[33]

Symphony No. 1 (1973) is an event in the career of the composer who has so far supported pure sonorism. It brings the subjugation of the sound element which is now subordinate to the logic of musical form, which in turn stems from the immersion of the composer in ancient culture: *Archē 1, Dýnamis 1, Dýnamis 2, Archē 2.* According to Teresa Malecka, the *Symphony* closes the stage of sonoristic thinking and opens the stage of musical thinking in Penderecki's career. "The Symphony wants to construct its world from scratch, according to a principle. It wants to construct it with the *archē*, thus it wants to tackle a grand topic."[34]

Magnificat (1974) could be considered a continuation of a series of grand works which dominated the previous phase. What is new here strikes the eye right after opening the score: the graphics have disappeared, notes are back, and the texture has become more dense than ever before. Now it is not only voices that are in counterpoint, but the entire clusters of voices. Through the ages the canticle from the New Testament has developed tradition contributed to by such diverse composers as Dufay and Mikołaj from Radom as well as Mikołaj Zieleński and Bach. Penderecki can be ascribed to the latter cantata–oratorio tradition. The praise of God is proclaimed in a solemn tone and in the monumental form, which is soon to become Penderecki's standard approach.

The Awakening of Jacob (1974), an instrumental splinter of the sound matter which led to the creation of *Magnificat.* Krzysztof Droba claimed to have heard in this music the idiom of the symphonic poem genre,[35] which was denied by the composer with a remark to the effect that the title and the Biblical motto have appeared over the notes quite accidentally. In any case, the score reveals the type of thinking that is more symphonic than orchestral.

The music given to us by Krzysztof Penderecki at the beginning of the 1970s seems to be of a quality that is subtle rather than explicit. The palette of expressive qualities has been refined and the counterpoint made twice as elaborate. The works from this period might be regarded as studies in tone color, articulation, nuances of dynamics. The form has become "packed," pervaded with imitation and variation principles, most frequently having the character of a passacaglia. But everything served one purpose: it was to allow for the unconstrained expression of the new lyricism, contemplation, exaltation, and ecstasy.

Time of Dialog With the Rediscovered Past, 1976–1985: the Phase of Paradise Lost

Even though here and there were signals of the arrival of the new style of Penderecki's, when it was actually revealed, first in the *Concerto for Violin* and then in *Paradise Lost* and *Symphony No. 2,* it astounded and shocked. The reference to the post–Romantic idiom was open, undisguised by the composer and not denied in interviews:

> I think that development does not just mean going forward; sometimes one must stop to think, retrace a couple of steps in order to be able to go forward.[36]

Once again Krzysztof Penderecki showed the courage to contradict the opinions of the scribes. Behind him he had his audiences and...Stravinsky. After all the author of *Oedipus Rex* and *Symphony of Psalms* did write in *Poetics of Music*:

> The true tradition is not the testimony to the past, it is a living power which stimulates and shapes the present.[37]

Penderecki did not hide his enthusiasm for the music of the end of the 19th century. He believed that this thread which was suddenly cut short has enough vitality to be continued; of course it was to be done on another plane, in full awareness of what happened later. He said yes to the return of melody, but the one which did not forget the purifying lesson given to it by dodecaphony and serialism. He accepted neotonality, but only through the prism of the structural thinking of the new counterpoint; he approved of new symphonism, but the one which appeared in the context of the harmonies discovered by sonorism.

Concerto No. 1 for Violin (1976), composed to honor Isaac Stern, went along the route marked by the works of Beethoven, Brahms and Tchaikovsky as far as the type of expression is concerned: it gave to the violinist the melodiousness and virtuosity, as well as the moments of meditation in solo cadences. "It is a grand, magnificent, decadent and Romantic concerto," concludes Joanna Wnuk–Nazarowa. "The work is immersed in the darkness of tragedy and suffering, in the circle of stuffy semitones, tritones and minor thirds; as a synthesis of the decadent styles of the past epochs, it is the masterpiece appropriate for our *fin de millēnaire*."[38]

Paradise Lost (1978), labeled by the composer a *sacra rappresentazione*, revealed the breadth of the sweeping new style, its lack of respect for time and the monumentalism of the forces, texture and form. But could the theme of the history of mankind, its fall and redemption be treated in any other way? The theme had been delineated by Milton but its interpretation was the task which the composer set himself. "Side by side with the text of the Puritan," he says, "I put the original text from the Bible, the *Dies irae* sequence and the Protestant chorale. I have never liked orthodoxies, synonymous with dogmatism and intolerance."[39] The fight of Satan with God and God with Satan over the fate of man takes place in front of the audience not only in the sphere of text; the music itself carries this weight, functioning symbolically through its sound patterns, which are loaded with meaning.[40] With closed eyes one is able to decide whether the world involved at any moment is human, divine or satanic. For the first time Penderecki allowed someone else's music to speak for him, and even more strongly so than his own music: in the disheveled, post–Romantic and sonoristic culmination he suddenly played Bach's chorale (*O grosse Lieb*). He spoke to us then no longer as the sound director or even a composer, but as an artist speaking on the matters of culture.

Symphony No. 2 "Christmas" (1980). Here, the music created earlier could be heard too, subtly and illusively carrying a symbolic message: this time it is the first four tones of the truly international Christmas carol *Silent Night, Holy Night*. From the viewpoint of harmony the sonoristic imagination of the work is immersed in the world of Wagner, Bruckner, and perhaps even Mahler and Sibelius. According to Joanna Wnuk–Nazarowa, we have in front of us the "projection of the musical passions of Krzysztof Penderecki." Or in other words: "not a distorting mirror of the 19th century symphonism, but its apotheosis."[41]

Te Deum (1980). Penderecki has always reacted as a barometer of the history of the world of man, particularly of the perilous moments in this history. *Te Deum* constituted his reaction to a favorable moment, and was dedicated to the Polish Pope in the year 1980, quite eventful for Poland.[42] Anna Oberc in her highly historical interpretation of the work, which she calls "a universal work, stretching beyond the framework of a single generation and a single nation, and still profoundly Polish,"[43] stresses the fact that *Te Deum* was completed only three weeks before the strikes in the Gdańsk shipyards began. In the Latin hymn constituting the culmination of the work, the *Boże coś Polske,* the anthem of those days[44] resounds, as if from afar, *quasi da lontano,* among the clamor of sounds.

Concerto No. 2 for Cello (1982), composed in honor of Mstisłav Rostropovich, the third approach to the theme, which was a successful contribution to the history of this rather unpopular genre. The work is an interplay between dramatism and brilliance, and hardly gives the soloist a moment's rest. The language which Penderecki employs to speak to us is easily recognizable as the language of the *Concerto for Violin* as well as *Symphony No. 2*: it is established and codified, and it does not bring surprises.

The Polish Requiem (1980–1984), the work of grandest conception and dimensions, growing over the years, and not yet completed[45], as if the composer was reluctant to put the final touches. There is no other work in Polish music which would be more deeply connected with history. And the history is quite recent. The work seems to prove the validity of the otherwise rather hyperbolic statement of Theodore W. Adorno that every truly great piece of art constitutes a reaction to the "horror of history." "I remember," recalls Penderecki, "that during the first performance of *Lacrimosa*,[46] which took place under the monument to the fallen shipyard workers of Gdańsk (1980), there were a million, maybe two million people on the square! It seems to me that in certain moments music is important and writing such a piece is perhaps more significant than writing an excellent string quartet."[47] At present the *Requiem* consists of eight main movements, among them the monumental *Dies Irae* which is further divided into eleven sections, differentiated according to their character and expression. The fervent soprano voice intoning *Lacrimosa* and the supporting choral voices remain long in the memory. But the moment which has the strongest appeal in *The Polish Requiem* is the occurrence of the supplications in Polish during the lamentative *Recordare* solo movement: the chant *Święty Boże, Święty Mocny* [Holy God, Holy and Mighty] resounds with calm and power.

The musical dialog with the past, rediscovered and taken to be his own, serves Penderecki as a means to express his attitude towards the events which he happens to witness. Penderecki's nature would not even conceive of adopting some "splendid isolation." He belongs to those who wish to and can participate in the happening of history. At times like that it would be difficult not to strike an emotional or even pathetic tone, it would be difficult to avoid creating a patriotic *theatrum*, which evokes connotations with the Baroque. There are moments when the imperatives turn up that are more pressing than just the wish to preserve the "purity" of the genre or the autonomy of the work of art.

AT THE THRESHOLD OF A NEW SYNTHESIS? 1985–1993: THE PHASE OF *THE BLACK MASK*

The leaf is turned over again and Penderecki remains himself, although perhaps he is not the same person any longer. He feels the necessity to liberate himself from the style in which he has stuck, in which writing started to be too easy. After the extensive, outward motion, there came a time of the intensity of means, of the focus on a more compact space, of the reduction of excess. Explaining the change of style, which became apparent when *The Black Mask* appeared on the opera stages of Salzburg, Vienna and Poznań, he says: "I wanted to depart from the monumentality of *sacra rappresentazione* which was proper for the period of my fascination with late Romanticism."[48]

Penderecki has always written many little works, the trifles, the *le petit rien*, such as *capriccia* and *cadenze*, for cello, viola or tuba, for oboe or violin. They often came into being on the fringe of grand, serious works, as if the splinters from them or their ludic counterpoints. Now more and more of these begin to appear, their form frequently rising in significance: *Song of Cherubim, Veni Creator, Benedictus* and *Benedicamus Domino* for a cappella choir, *Per Slava* for cello, *Preludio* for solo clarinet, *Der unterbrochene Gedanke* for string quartet. And the works composed in the forms which are intrinsically broader, such as a trio, quartet, concerto or symphony, become less eloquent, more compact or more ephemeral. It is quite understandable that in the period concerned, the works that received the most attention, evoked the greatest admiration or caused the most profound astonishment were *The Black Mask* and *Ubu Rex*.

> *The Black Mask* (1986), an outstanding, deeply moving work, placed by many critics side by side with Richard Strauss's *Salome* and Alban Berg's *Wozzeck*. Masterly constructed, almost bursting out from the abundance of material, and still extraordinarily concise. The starting point of the opera was the late (1929), forgotten drama of a German expressionist playwright, Gerhardt Hauptmann; there, in the words of Wolfram Schwinger, "the distinct reality of the surrealistic",[49] which had always fascinated the

composer, came to the fore. Penderecki himself confesses: "After I had read Hauptmann, it seemed to me that the entire play, apart from the finale which I have changed, was one grand Baroque *danse macabre*, the combination of the morbid and the farcical."[50] He was fascinated, as he says further on, by the very structure of the drama, the complete unity of action, time and space, the placing at one table of a Jew, a Huguenot, a Jansenist, a Lutheran pastor and a Catholic abbot. All of them, except Perl, the Wandering Jew, are drawn into the dance of death which leads them to perdition. Penderecki gives a surprisingly detailed account of his composing procedure. First, the citations appeared, which brought the authenticity of time and space into this surrealistic crime story: the Glockenspiel melody, a couple of chorales, the feasting music, then the counterpoints of these which constitute the immediate sound matter of the work are organized and ruled by the peculiar tonal structure and the rhythm, which is a new element in Penderecki's music. The rhythm of the form develops and keeps returning in front of our eyes in a crazy pace and with rigid consistency.

The Song of Cherubim (1986), dedicated to Mstisław Rostropovich, although written in the period dominated by the expressive gloominess of *The Black Mask*, emerges as the sanctuary and oasis of contemplation, light and peace. Penderecki has again referred to Orthodox chants and climate in order to flash open a metaphysical perspective before his friend and the audience.

Veni Creator (1987) for a cappella choir was composed by Penderecki for the city of Madrid, whose university had just granted him an honorary doctorate. Another oasis of solemnity, trust and calm, drawn with a firm hand of the master of the choral texture.

Symphony No. 4 (1989), and, in fact, its first movement, *Adagio*. The composer was invited to take part in the festivities commemorating the French Revolution. Despite the probable expectations, he wrote neither a cantata on the virtues of Robespierre nor an ode in honor of the guillotine, but a work dominated by the serious, reflective tone.

Ubu Rex (1991), an opera buffa in 2 acts with a prologue and an epilogue. It might have seemed that the scandalizing text of a fourteen–year–old youngster and his naughty pals, which outraged the French public so much at the turn of the century, had gone down in history in the chapter called *camera obscura*. Penderecki was tempted several times to bring the little play of Alfred Jarry's to light again, at least as an antidote to his own scores, mostly devoted to noble and sublime ideas. Already in 1963 he tape–recorded some brass band tune, which accompanied the puppet interpretation of a text in some theater in Stockholm. Now he painstakingly composed a large–scale work, into which he put his entire wit, his genuine sense of humor and love of paradox, the extraordinary ability to overhear and mock the musical styles and mannerisms, and the craft of carrying a contrapuntal dialog with himself in the *serio* and *buffo* modes. And maybe he also wished to get up the nose of those who tired him with their high expectations? What has resulted is a hybrid work, which can swing towards the grotesque or the macabre, the pathetic *buffo* or the operatic cabaret, depending on the approach taken by the director and the stage manager. The music itself is a reference to "postmodern memory", which helps us decipher Penderecki's play with consecutive conventions, from these of Rossini to those of Wagner and Prokofiev, and makes us laugh, or at least smile. The first Munich performance of the opera did not cause a scandal nor has it outraged anyone. We live in the world in which showing the absurd, the stupid or the vulgar, the aggressive or the cruel in a playful context, is not considered relevant to the sphere of ethics.

Symphony No. 5 (1992) dedicated to the audiences from the Far East, and called "Korean," brings the music which is condensed and highly dramatic in its expression, and uses the instrumentation which mobilizes imagination, perhaps taking its inspiration from the oriental. And it is perhaps for the first time in Penderecki's works that the symphonic spirit of Mahler has resonated so strongly.

Sinfonietta Per Archi (1992), the music, written on a rather light note, is transparent, compact, highly logically constructed, resembling the idiom of neoclassical orchestras of the 1920s. The grotesque parts seem to testify to the closeness of *Ubu Rex.*

Concerto for Flute and Chamber Orchestra (1992) transports us into the realm of the classical, and perhaps the ancient, the Virgilian, the bucolic and the Mediterranean. One would wish to say that the flute presents its motives here and spins its sound arabesques in the open, airy and radiant space. It livens up only in order to fall into a nostalgic or elegiac reflection a moment afterwards. It takes up a dialog with a "tree" and awakens from the dreamy meditation upon a sudden invasion of kettledrums, the brass and the strings, articulated in Bartók's vein. The deep shade of double basses prepares us for the partly expected, but still surprising euphony of the final chord.

Quartet for Clarinet and Strings (1993) reveals to us the Penderecki who has finally left *Ubu Rex* behind him. Here, just as in the *Sinfonietta,* the clear structure of the four–movement work stems from the high economy of musical means. There is not a single tone of clarinet, violin, viola or cello which is not dictated by the absolute contrapuntal necessity. The work rises with the *pianissimo* in the *Adagio*, and sets with the *pianissimo* in the *Larghetto*, bursting with the *vivacissimo* of the *scherzo* and the *grazioso* of the *serenade* in between. The categories of expression which remain in the memory are the reflection, lyricism, life and beauty.

Following Penderecki's career closely, from one work to the next, from one phase to another, one notices how purely instrumental works intermingle with vocal ones, those written in the *serio* style with those verging on the *buffo*. Just like in the Book of *Qoheleth*[51]: there is a time to be silent and a time to speak, a time to weep and a time to laugh.... The latest phase has brought along the greatest variety, it even seems to have the character of a *stretta* of the contradictory qualities. Penderecki attacks in various directions, experiences various types of matter. But all along he has had the awareness of living and working at the time of the new Tower of Babel. Hence his further awareness: that of the necessity of a synthesis. This is the theme that insistently keeps appearing in his recent statements:

> The need for a synthesis is characteristic for the whole modern epoch (it covers the 19th and the 20th centuries). This is the response to the poignant feeling of the disintegration of the world.[52]

It would be a catastrophic awareness if it was not accompanied by the sense of faith in the possibility of fighting disintegration, primarily though a synthesis.

> It seems to me, that what has the chance of survival is only the music which is written in a natural way and constitutes a synthesis of everything that has happened in the last few decades[53].

To put it more directly: such a synthesis consists in "the absorption of everything that has occurred before."[54]

This sounds as a program and it is this very program that Penderecki seems to be implementing in his artistic work. And he clearly does not mean to produce stylistic conglomerates, but rather the new unities, born out of the high temperature of experiencing the chosen and rejecting the accidental. The new formula of Penderecki's also affects the building of structures: his music has rehabilitated the refrain and the reprise, the anticipation and the stretta, that is, everything that contributes to unity.

Moreover, Penderecki counteracts the disintegration of art and the world with the argument, which he perhaps most clearly articulated in the speech at the University of Poznań in 1987; there he talked about the necessity to go back to the values carelessly lost or abandoned under pressure, having in mind the traditions based on the *sacrum*[55].

How are we going to be surprised or delighted by Krzysztof Penderecki tomorrow? We know of one project which has been maturing for years: a Christmas oratorio. But let us perhaps not count the chickens before they are hatched.

NOTES

1. From Krzysztof Penderecki's conversation with Anna and Zbigniew Baran, "Passio artis et vitae" [Passion for art and life], *Dekada Literacka* 1:11/ 12, May/June, 1992, p. 4.
2. When it was incorporated into Austria.
3. Officially a Polish sporting society, but in fact a national paramilitary, anti–Austrian organization (Sokół=falcon).
4. Normally, a four–year school.
5. Krzysztof Penderecki at a seminar in Cracow in January, 1975, *Muzyka* 2 (1976), p. 29–52.
6. *Dziady*, by Adam Mickiewicz (1823), one of the most famous Polish Romantic (and patriotic) dramas; *Chłopi*, by W.S. Reymont, a realistic novel on the rural life, for which the author received a Nobel Prize in 1924.
7. *Nie–boska Komedia* (lit. The Un–divine Comedy), by Z. Krasiński (1835), one of the three principal Polish Romantic poets.
8. *La Comédie humaine*, by Honoré Balzac.
9. 1893–1970, a well–known Polish philosopher, one of the main representatives of phenomenology.
10. Krzysztof Penderecki, "Passio artis et vitae", *op. cit.*, p. 4.
11. See the list of works of Penderecki's in the Appendix to the present volume.
12. The greatest Polish Renaissance poet (1530–84).
13. The Society of Polish Composers (Związlzek Kompozytorów Polskich).
14. Krzysztof Penderecki, "Muzyki nie można zaczynać od pocziątku" [Music cannot be started afresh], *Ruch muzyczny* 22 (1987), p. 3.
15. Krzysztof Penderecki, "Passion artis et vitae", *op. cit.*, p. 4.
16. Krzysztof Penderecki,"Passio artis et vitae", *op. cit.*, p. 4.
17. Krzysztof Droba, "Kwartety smyczkowe" [String quartets] In: *Festiwal Muzyki Krzysztofa Pendereckiego. Kraków, Lusławice, Poznań, 9–16 VI 1988*, Kraków, 1988, p. 31.
18. Tadeusz A. Zielinski, "Nowe utwory Krzysztofa Pendereckiego" [New works by Krzysztof Penderckil], *Ruch Muzyczny* 1 (1961), p. 17.
19. Karl H. Wörner, "Donaueschingen 1960—bez sensacji" Donaueschingen 1960—without sensation], *Ruch Muzyczny* 1 (1961), p. 12–13.

20. Ludwik Erhardt, *Spotkania z Krzysztofem Pendereckim* [Conversations wtih Krzysztof Penderecki] (Krakow: PWM, 1975), p. 58–59.

21. Krzysztof Penderecki in an interview given in Münster on 30 March 1966, on the occasion of the first performance of *The Passion*. Cited after Ludwik Erhardt, *Spotkania, op.cit.*, p. 89.

22. An interview with Krzysztof Penderecki, "Sukces jest podejrzany", *Polityka* 15 (1985), p. 1, 9.

23. Krzysztof Penderecki, "Passio artis et vitae", *op.cit.*, p. 4.

24. Krzysztof Penderecki, *Dies irae* (Kraków: PWM, 1969)

25. Władysław Broniewski (1897–1962), Polish poet, most famous for his pre–World War II revolutionary poetry.

26. Tadeusz Różewicz, Polish poet and playwright, best known for dramatic post–war lyrics and plays.

27. *Figaro Littéraire* 9–15 Dec 1968. Cited after Ludwig Erhardt, *Spotkania, op.cit.,* p. 106.

28. Krzysztof Penderecki, "Passio artis et vitae", *op.cit.*, p. 5.

29. "Matka Joanna od Aniołów" — a short story by J. Iwaszkiewicz (1946), screened by J. Kawalerowicz (1961).

30. A. David Hogarth, "The Truth and the Paradox," *Philips Music Record*, Summer 1970. Cited after Ludwig Erhardt, *Spotkania, op. cit.*, p. 128.

31. Krzysztof Penderecki, "Muzyki nie można zaczynać od początku", *op. cit.*, p. 3.

32. Krzysztof Penderecki, "Kulturotwórcza moc chrześcijaństwa", *Tygodnik Powszechny* 1 (1988), p. 3.

33. Barbara Cisowska, "W kręgu *Canticum canticorum*" [in the circle of *Canticum canticorum* In: Teresa Malecka (ed) *Księga jubileuszowa Mieczysława Tomaszewskiego*, Kraków 1984, p. 158–202.

34. Teresa Malecka, "I Symfonia," In: *Współczesność i tradycja w muzyce K. Pendereckiego (Kraków: Akademia Muzyczna, 1983)*, pp. 176–186.

35. Krzysztof Droba, "Przebudzenie Jakuba," In: Leszek Polony (ed.), *Muzyka w kontekście kutury. Spotkania muzyczne w Baranowie, 1 (1976)*, Kraków 1978, pp. 67–72.

36. An interview with Krzysztof Penderecki, "Sukces jest podejrzany", *op. cit.*

37. Igor Stravinsky, "Poetyka muzyczna", *Res Facta* 4 (1970), p. 198–225.

38. Joanna Wnuk–Nazarowa, "O Koncercie skrzypcowym Pendereckiego" In: *Księga jubileuszowa M. Tomaszewskiego* (Kraków 1984), p. 78.

39. Krzysztof Penderecki, "Passio artis et vitae", *op. cit.* p. 5.

40. Regina Chłopicka, "*Raj utracony*. Sacra rappresentazione K. Pendereckiego" In: *Dramat i teatr sakralny*. KUL, Lublin 1988, p. 189–207.

41. Joanna Wnuk–Nazarowa, "II Symfonia 'Wigilijna'" [Symphony No. 2 "Christmas"] [in:] *Festiwal*..., 1988, *op. cit.* , p. 26.

42. In August 1980 Lech Wałęsa signed the agreement with the Polish government and the Solidarity trade union was formed.

43. Anna Oberc, "Te Deum" In: *Wspołczesność i tradycja*..., *op. cit.*, p. 263.

44. The religious supplicatory hymn sung in Polish churches, in the 1980's usually accompanied by the show of hands with a "V" sign, in defiance of the Communist establishment.

45. According to the composer's statement from 1993, with the completion of "Sanctus" (1993), *The Polish Requiem* has acquired its last and final part.

46. The work is often spelled "Lacrimosa."

47. Krzysztof Penderecki in the interview "Sukces jest podejrzany", *op. cit.*

48. Krzysztof Penderecki, "Passio artis et vitae", *op. cit.*, p. 5.

49. Wolfram Schwinger, *Krzysztof Penderecki. Begegnungen. Lebensdaten. Werkkommentare* (Stuttgart, 1979).

50. Krzysztof Penderecki, "Passio artis et vitae", *op. cit.*, p. 5.

51. Better known as the Ecclesiastes.

52. Krzysztof Penderecki, "Passio artis et vitae", *op. cit.*, p. 4.

53. Krzysztof Penderecki, "Muzyki nie można zaczynać od początku", *op. cit.*, p. 2.

54. Krzysztof Penderecki, "Kulturotwórcza moc chrzescijanstwa," *Tygodnik Powszechny* 1 (1988), p. 3.

Translated by Władysław Grzegorz Chłopicki

Ray Robinson

WEST PALM BEACH

Penderecki's Musical Pilgrimage

> The stages of my development as a composer are fairly distinct. After the period of search, up to *Stabat mater*, I simplified my musical language, next I turned to tradition, the Netherlands schools to polyphony and counterpoint—that would be my second period. The latest includes *Partita, Magnificat, Jacob's Awakening*, and the *Violin Concerto* [No. 1] which I have just completed.[1]

When a composer reaches the milestone of his sixth decade the question of style periods begins to become a logical part of the inquiry into his compositional achievements. Actually the subject of style changes in Penderecki's music became an issue as early as 1962 when the a cappella choral work *Stabat mater* first appeared and signalled such a radical departure from the modern, avant–garde oriented "sonoristic" works of his post–student years (1958–62). Since that point in his career, each new composition has been analyzed by critics and Penderecki scholars alike for evidence relating to its stylistic characteristics. Understandably there is not complete agreement between the composer and theorists on this issue, nor should there be. The creator and scholar have radically different roles in the musical art. One can only imagine the response a scholar might have received had he asked a composer like Mozart, Beethoven or Berlioz to discuss the style periods in their works. Penderecki finds it amusing that scholars would even attempt this type of exercise.

When asked in 1977 to trace the evolution of his style up to that point in his career, Penderecki clearly outlined three periods:

> I think the first period of my development would be from *Anáklasis* and *Threnody*, the first compositions written in my style. . . . until after I finished *Fluorescences*.
>
> So, in 1962, I backtracked a little and wrote *Stabat mater*. I didn't know which way to go at that time, and I wasn't sure that what I was doing was really right. Maybe I had gone too far and there was no way back. . . so *Stabat mater* is the beginning of the second period, I would say. The second period lasted until 1973, because that is when I finished the Sym-

> phony [No. 1]. . . [a work] which was important for me because it was the first large piece I wrote for orchestra.
>
> I think the third period begins with the *Awakening of Jacob* and the *Magnificat*, and maybe *Ecloga*. In 1972 and 1973 there are some changes in my thinking which I developed after *Ecloga* and *Magnificat*.[2]

It is significant that the composer has identified *Anáklasis* and *Threnody* as "the first compositions written in his [emphasis mine] style." It is also noteworthy that he considers *Stabat mater* and the *Awakening of Jacob* as "landmark" pieces; in each case the style is so radically different from the compositions that precede them. Six years later the same question was raised in another interview and Penderecki's thoughts on the subject had changed somewhat in the intervening period. In 1983, Penderecki felt that there were now two, not three, style periods in his music:

> I rather think now that there are two style periods in my career as a composer. I do not count the very beginning pieces like *Strophes*, which were written before I really started to develop my own language as a composer. The first period, I would say, was from *Anáklasis* and *Threnody*, which were the first pieces I could call my music, until maybe the *Awakening of Jacob*; I would say *Magnificat* was the last piece in that style...The *Awakening of Jacob* opened the second period. It has elements of both [periods], of course.[3]

Ten years later the question was raised once more by this writer and predictably the answer was a little different. When queried about the same issue in the summer of 1993, Penderecki suggested that there was really only one style in his music. It was his opinion that the musical language he had developed in the early years of his career was still the basic material of his art. Even as his music became more conservative after the *Awakening of Jacob* in 1974, he argued, certain elements of his early style (i.e. experimental time notation, clusters, glissandi, instumental effects, micro–tones, percussion instruments, etc.) continued to play an integral role in his musical language.[4]

So it is fairly evident from these interviews that Penderecki recognizes two major stylistic adjustments in his career as a composer, even if he will no longer admit to clearly–definable style periods: (1) the look back to tradition as evidenced in the style characteristics of *Stabat mater* (1962) and *St. Luke Passion* (1965–66); and (2) the change in 1974 to a more expressive, even "romantic" style as found first in the *Awakening of Jacob*, and then in works of which the *Violin Concerto* (1976–77), the opera *Paradise Lost* (1975–78) and

Symphony No. 2 are representative. The fact that he now recognizes consistent elements in his musical language is significant. We will have more to say about this later in this essay.

It is, therefore, the purpose of this article to explore Penderecki's musical pilgrimage in some detail in order to develop a systematic basis for the identification of stylistic changes in his works. We will begin with the problems one faces when attempting this task.

PROBLEMS IN TRACING PENDERECKI'S STYLISTIC DEVELOPMENT

First of all, the stylistic changes in the music of Penderecki are difficult to place in a strict chronological order because of the overlapping that occurs among and between them. In short, his works do not fall into neat categories. For example, even though the choral work *Stabat mater* initiated a significant style change in 1962, many of the "modern" characteristics of the works of his early period are still apparent in works as late as 1974 (*i.e. De natura sonoris* No. 1: 1966; *Symphony No. 1*: 1973; and *Magnificat*: 1974), although there is a tendency toward a more linear style in the works composed after 1972. So the first problem that must solved when seeking to organize the composer's creative work into defensible categories is to recognize and deal with this overlapping.

The second difficulty is the composer's tendency to approach his art in a dynamic rather than static manner. When one looks at some of the so–called "modern" characteristics of Penderecki's musical language—*i.e.*, the search for new sonorities—it is difficult to limit ones findings to the early and mid–1960s. For instance, it is possible to identify at least two periods of experimentation in his work: (1) the search for new instrumental sonorities and novel effects with stringed instruments and electronic sounds in the works of the early 1960s; and (2) the experimentation with types of vocal sonorities and melodic writing in the 1970's. We must also take note of the electronic tape piece *Ekecheiría* (1972), which appears more than ten years after he abandons work in the Experimental Electronic Studio in Warsaw. Composed for the opening ceremony of the 1972 Olympic Games in Munich, Germany, it only supports the argument that Penderecki's compositional style is dynamic rather than static.

The third difficulty in assigning specific periods to his music is the eclectic nature of the works themselves. As stated by Mieczysław Tomaszewski in 1988, Penderecki "is interested in everything ... the full abundance,"[5] in any musical device that will express a specific musical idea. Hence we find a mixture of stylistic elements in all periods and phases of his writing except in the years of his "sonoristic" compositions (1959–62). The coloristic use of the orchestra in both *Threnody* in the early years and then in the *Polish Requiem*, long after he had turned his attention to matters other than "sonorism"; or the use of sonoristic devices in *De natura sonoris No. 1* and the *Symphony No. 1*, a number of years after the end of his so–called "sonoristic" period, are examples of this quality in his music.

So it is quite obvious that the compositional career of Penderecki does not lend itself to strict and easily definable periods. When we create them, we are establishing arbitrary guidelines that should not be too rigid. There are, however, certain works that signal clear changes in style and these must be identified and evaluated for their relevance in this analysis. By Penderecki's own admission, "the pure Netherlands style of *Stabat mater*" and the distinct "atmospheric" quality in *The Awakening of Jacob* are two such compositions. The composer himself, in the interview excerpts above, has singled out these as landmark works that reveal a clear adjustment of style. *Anáklasis*, the *Violin Concerto No. 1* and the opera *Ubu Rex*, we believe, are three other works that signify new directions in his work. Therefore, in an effort to present a thorough analysis, we have approached the problem on three levels: by creating style phases (the micro–form level); by melding these phases into style periods (the macro–form level) and then by identifying common elements in all phases and periods of the composer's career (the conceptual level). We will begin by discussing Penderecki's style phases.

IDENTIFYING PENDERECKI'S STYLE PHASES

This problem has been approached by applying nine traditional elements of musical style and measuring them against the musical characteristics we find in the composer's musical language. The elements are: a) rhythm, b) pitch, c) linear events, d) vertical structure, e) tonality, f) texture, g) form, h) instrumentation, i) and extra–musical influences. In each style phase we have also sought to identify an exemplary work which contains elements of that phase. By using this process, six phases in Penderecki's pilgrimage have been identified.

PHASE ONE—THE SEARCH FOR A NEW MUSICAL LANGUAGE (1956–59)

Penderecki's public career as a composer begins with his first published work: *Miniatures for Clarinet* (1956). This piece was composed while he was still at student at the Academy of Music in Cracow. Phase One includes the *Psalms of David*, *Emanations* for Two String Orchestras, *Miniatures* for Violin and Piano and *Strophes*. This phase is characterized by the composer's initial search for a personal style: each work is an exercise in his developing compositional technique. All these works are published and some, like the *Psalms of David*, still receive regular performances. *Strophes* is considered the exemplar work in this first phase.

a. Rhythm: There is experimentation with a three line speed–graph notation in *Strophes*. This practice continues with *Anáklasis* but is abandoned thereafter.
b. Pitch: The pitch basis is traditional with some experiments in tuning (*i.e. Emanations*) where the two orchestras are tuned a minor second apart.
c. Linear events: There are experiments with serialism in these years. For example, there is a clear attempt at twelve–tone writing in the second movement of *Psalms of David*; the practice of "melodic" writing that is characterized by minor seconds, tritones and octave displacement begins here. This type of linear expression will become a Penderecki "signature".
d. Vertical structures: In this phase there are traditional intervals as well as experiments with diatonic and chromatic clusters.
e. Tonality: These works are atonal with some references to a tonal center.
f. Texture: There is a mixture in this phase with delicately–balanced and refined sonorities of voices and instruments (*Psalms of David*) mixed with experiments in pointillistic textures (*Strophes*) .
g. Form: closed and through–composed structures
h. Instrumentation: chamber–sized forces
i. Extra–musical influences: the text of *Strophes* (from Menander, Sophocles, Isaiah, Jeremiah and Omar Khayyam) gives the work a metaphysical quality.

Phase Two—Experiments with instrumental sonorities (1959–67)

This phase in the composer's style can be defined as "sonoristic" in that the "sound coloristic" element of the style functions as the primary factor of the composition. The first work in this style is *Anáklasis*, followed by *Dimensions of Time and Silence*, *Threnody*, *String Quartet No. 1*, *Fonogrammi* for Flute and Chamber Orchestra, *Polymorphia*, *Canon* for String Orchestra and Two Tape Recorders, and *Fluorescences*. Later compositions which might be considered "sonoristic" are *De natura sonoris* No. 1, *Capriccio* for Violin and Orchestra, *String Quartet No. 2*, *De natura sonoris* No. 2 and *Symphony No. 1*. *Threnody to the Victims of Hiroshima* is undoubtedly the exemplar work in this style phase. The compositional elements include:

a. Rhythm: three–line tempo graph in *Anáklasis*, space–time notation in *Threnody* and later works. The rhythmic basis of these works is non–traditional.
b. Pitch: sonoristic pitch notation, defined pitches in dense clusters, microtones, glissandi

c. Linear events: melody as such does not exist. The composer creates linear events out of electro–cardiagram printouts which are developed as "sound events" (*i.e. Polymorphia*).
d. Vertical structures: various types of clusted events are developed by the composer; "stationary clusters" (*Threnody*), "glissandi" clusters (*Anáklasis*), "rotating" clusters (*Polymorphia*). One of the most stunnning examples is the dense thirty second, 52 voice micro–tonal cluster that comes at the end of *Threnody*.
e. Tonality: atonal. It should be noted that the composer experiments with major chord endings in works like *Polymorphia*, which ends in a bright "C" major chord, to bring release to the tension he has created with the dense atonal texture.
f. Texture: bold, broad bands of sound alternate with highly organized, serially–conceived sections, climaxed in a 36–part canon in pointillistic textures in *Threnody*.
g. Form: sectional forms related to sonositic events; (i.e. rounded–binary form) in *Threnody*.
h. Instrumentation: large string orchestra (*Threnody*), large orchestra with extensive percussion battery (*Fluorescences*).
i. Extra–musical influences: The dedication of *Threnody* to the "Victims of Hiroshima" (even though after the fact) gives the work a universal, humanistic quality

Phase Three—The synthesis of this sonoristic language with traditional musical elements (1962–72)

At this point in his creative life Penderecki looks back to tradition for inspiration. One of the most interesting aspects of this phase is the melding of his modern, avant–garde style with traditional forms (polyphonic motet in *Stabat mater*, passacaglia in the *Passion*, orthodox liturgy in *Utrenya*). Some of the works which fall within this phase: *Stabat mater, St. Luke Passion, Dies irae, Devils of Loudun, Utrenya,* and *Cosmogony*. The *St. Luke Passion* is without doubt the exemplar work in this style phase. The style elements include:

a. Rhythm: standard metrical sections alternated with space–time notation and free rhythmic passages.
b. Pitch: standard pitch notation in the chorus is mixed with micro–tonal writing in the orchestra and soloists. Sonoristic devices like highest possible note and lowest possible note continue in orchestral instruments.
c. Linear events: "melodic" writing in the *Passion* emanates from two tone rows (called Cantus Firmus I and Cantus Firmus II by the composer). B–A–C–H motive, *Święty Boże* motive and *Stabat mater* theme

give the work a "serial" quality. Other melodic devices are found in the microtones, diatonic writing and modality, etc.

d. Vertical structures: dense cluster chords alternate with traditional chord structures (last chord in *Stabat mater* and final chorus in *Passion* both end in bright major chord sonorities). The composer states that the purpose is to release tension.

e. Tonality: atonal. There is reference to tonal centers from time to time but not in the sense that they become a specific reference point in the tonality.

f. Texture: eclectic mixture of styles

g. Form: sectional, usually by text in the choral works (*i.e., St Luke Passion* is divided into two main parts and 27 sections or movements); the composer uses earlier form models as references (*i.e.,* the passacaglia in "Popule meus", No. 16 in the *Passion).*

h. Instrumentation: large orchestra, two and three choirs, boy choir, large percussion battery, soloists and narrator in choral works of this phase.

i. Extra–musical influences: Biblical narrative is given universal symbolism by composer in press conference at premiere. Work is "the suffering and death of Christ, but it is also the suffering and death at Auschwitz, the tragic experience of mankind in the middle of the twentieth century."[7] It is therefore symbolic of similar events which have occurred in contemporary culture.

Phase Four—The phase of stylistic sophistication: experiments with vocal sonorities, complicated polyphonic and melodic writing (1972–74)

Mieczysław Tomasczewski has called these years in the creative life of the composer "a phase of transition,"[8] while we would prefer to name them a second phase of "search and experimentation." However this time the search is for vocal sonorities and linear devices as the primary objects. This phase produces the composer's most sophisticated writing. Penderecki gives a clue to the advanced quality of these works when he says:

> I think of the two pieces, pieces which I wrote in 1973–74—*Canticum canticorum Salomonis* and *Magnificat.* I believe it is almost impossible to perform these pieces properly with all the quarter tones that I wrote. In these two works I reached the point where I could not go forward and continue the same style. The technique was all over me, overwhelming me.[9]

This writer would add *Ecloga VIII* (1972) to this list. Instrumental writing continues during these years and produces the *Symphony No. 1.*

The composer has called *Awakening of Jacob* a "landmark" work in the evolution of his compositional technique. The atmosphere created in the opening measures by the shimmering and tentative sound of 12 ocarinas punctuated in a non–metric rhythmic texture by quiet, widely–spaced cluster chords in the low brass, produced sonorities that were very new for the composer. The work undoubtedly marked a dramatic change in style, not unlike that created in 1962 by the appearance of *Stabat mater.* Yet, make no mistake about it, this is still a modern, sonoristic piece with the same kind of experimental approach found in the earlier years. Consequently we have chosen to place this work in Phase Four since it is still a piece in which the composer is "searching", in this case for a more expressive style that ultimately comes "full bloom" in the *Violin Concerto No. 1.* The *Awakening of Jacob* thus paves the way for this new direction.

Other compositions which fall within this phase include the *Cello Concerto No. 1*, *Partita*, *Ecloga VIII*, and *Canticum canticorum Salomonis*, all highly sophisticated works that are "experimental" in their own way. *Magnificat* is the exemplary work. The stylistic characteristics of this phase include:

a. Rhythm: traditional metrical signatures mixed with space–time notation and freely rhythmic passages
b. Pitch: micro–tones mixed with traditional elements
c. Linear events: the linear interval of the minor third is introduced in *Ecloga VIII*, *Magnificat* and the *Awakening of Jacob.*
d. Vertical structures: clusters resulting from complicated, indeterminate writing alternate with clear moments where the major chord appears twice (*i.e. Magnificat*). The "Penderecki Chord" (major–minor triad with an additional tritone in the bass) appears first in *Magnificat.*
e. Tonality: atonal with major chords for release in *Magnificat*: E–flat major on the word "Gloria;" C major on the final chord
f. Texture: thoroughly eclectic works with extensive, highly complicated linear writing, indeterminate instrumental and vocal textures
g. Form: sectional with movements organized according to scriptural (liturgical) texts; traditional forms are inserted (*i.e.* clear example of fugal writing in "*Quia respexit*").
h. Instrumentation: large orchestra, heavy percussion battery, large chorus, male vocal sonorities explored with counter–tenors.
i. Extra–musical influences: inspiration from the biblical text, the ancient "Song of Mary" in Luke 1:46–55.

Phase Five—Synchronization of a more expressive musical language with the elements of the modern style (1975–86)

This phase, which has been called neo–romantic by some writers because of the expressive linear character of the melodic lines, emerges with the opera *Paradise Lost*, and includes the *Violin Concerto No. 1*, *Symphony No. 2*, *Te Deum*, *Concerto for Violoncello No. 1*, *Concerto for Viola* and *Polish Requiem*. The exemplary work is the *Violin Concerto No. 1*. The stylistic characteristics of this phase include:

a. Rhythm: return of traditional meter–tempo–rhythmic devices; characteristic "non–metrical" inserts that create tension and release
b. Pitch: traditional notation mixed with micro–tones in linear passages (in solo violin and string parts)
c. Melody: freely atonal "themes" that are serially conceived and based on three–note sets in a kind of twelve tone organization. The pattern "set" followed by "tri–tone" and octave displacement is typical. Interval class 1 predominates.
d. Harmony: traditional vertical textures alternate with clusters built on pitches from Interval Class 1. One vertical sonority that keeps appearing in these works (*Violin Concerto No. 1*, *Te Deum* and the opera *Paradise Lost*) is the "major–minor chord with tritone in the bass," the so–called "Penderecki chord."
e. Tonality: atonal with references to a pitch center
f. Texture: symphonic in conception with linear, polyphonic and sonoristic events
g. Form: one movement sectional form is the most popular (the opera *Die schwarze Maske* is composed in one act form) even in the large form works (*i.e.* *Violin Concerto No. 1*, *Symphony No. 2*, etc.).
h. Instrumentation: large orchestra, normal percussion, harp
i. Extra–musical influences: symbolic references to traditional forms of the 19th century (*i.e.* symphony, concerto, etc.). "I am only continuing a tradition," stated the composer in 1983.[10]

Phase Six—Stabilization of a mature expressive musical language with modern elements (1986–).

After the *Polish Requiem* and *Die schwarze Maske*, a series of works emerge which reveal an inclination to compose for smaller forces (orchestral and choral) and with more concise formal models. Chamber works and small choral pieces begin to appear after 1986. There is also less emphasis in this phase on the large percussion battery for its coloristic purposes. Not since his student days has Penderecki composed so many pieces for solo instrument and chamber ensemble (*i.e.* *Per Slava* for cello solo, *Preludium* for solo clarinet, *Der unterbrochene Gedanke* for string quartet, *String Trio* and *Quartet for Clarinet and String Trio)*. Another characteristic of this period is the appearance of a group of small form choral pieces: *Cherubim Song*, *Veni Creator*, *Benedicamus*

Domino for Men's Chorus, *Benedictus* and a second *Agnus Dei* for mixed chorus and chamber orchestra. This is also the period that produced Symphonies 3, 4, and 5.

The first major work in this new style phase is *Passacaglia and Rondo* for Orchestra, later incorporated into *Symphony No. 3*; *Adagio* for Orchestra (*Symphony No. 4*); the opera *Ubu Rex*; *String Trio* and its successor the popular *Sinfonietta No. 1* for string orchestra (the same work rearranged for string orchestra); *Concerto for Flute and Chamber Orchestra*; *Symphony No. 5*; *Quartet for Clarinet and String Trio*, and its successor the *Sinfonietta No. 2* (1996) for clarinet and string orchestra (the same work rearranged); *Entrata* for Brass and Timpani; and *Symphony No. 3*. *Ubu Rex* is the exemplary work. The stylistic features of this phase include:

a. Rhythm: traditional metric structure with a strong rhythmic element created by motor rhythms in changing meters and strong accentuations. Passages of free rhythm are inserted for tension and release.
b. Pitch: predominantly traditional with inserts of characteristic devices.
c. Linear events: themes based on free atonality; chromatic scalar figures dominate linear line; predilection for intervals of minor second and tri–tone; motivic development.
d. Vertical structures: very few traditional chords; vertical events in *Ubu Rex* are based on superimposed chains of fifths. Dissonant intervals of seconds, sevenths and ninths predominate, juxtaposed with the empty sounds of open fifths.
e. Tonality: atonal with references to tonal center (i.e. *Sinfonietta* where both G and D are referenced as "centers").
f. Texture: more transparent than in earlier phases, especially in *Ubu Rex*, chamber works and small choral pieces.
g. Form: *opera buffo*, through–composed form according to the scenes of the libretto. A dramatic structure in which the plot flows is punctuated by a constantly accelerating rhythm of successive tensions and climaxes. Penderecki once stated that he could not write a comic opera until the political situation in Poland had changed. It is significant that he finally completed *Ubu Rex* in 1990, one year after the fall of the Soviet Union.
h. Instrumentation: medium sized pit orchestra, 15–piece stage orchestra, large percussion section.
i. Extra–musical influences: the universal theme of political ethical values is found in the opera *Ubu Rex*.

Chart 1 presents a summary of the composer's stylistic characteristics in the six phases just discussed: (1) [search] the initial search for a new musical language (1956–59); (2) [sonority] the experiments with instrumental techniques

Chart I
Musical Elements in Penderecki's Style Phases

Macro Form Chart

Elements	Phase I (1956–1959)	Phase II (1959–1967)	Phase III (1962–1972)	Phase IV (1972–1974)	Phase V (1975–1986)	Phase VI (1986–)
Style Period	Search	Sonorism	Synthesis	Sophistication	Synchronization	Stabilization
Exemplar Work	Strophes	Threnody	St. Luke Passion	Magnificat	Violin Concerto No. 1	Ubu Rex
Rhythm	Speed–graph notation	Space–time notation	Space–time notation	Mixture of metric elements	Traditional metric notation	Traditional metric notation
Pitch	Traditional	Microtones	Microtones	Mixture	Traditional	Traditional
Linear events	Serialism	Free Atonality	Free Atonality	Free Atonality	Free Atonality	Free Atonality
Vertical structures	Traditional structures	Dense clusters	Dense clusters	"Signature" chord	Mixture	Mixture
Tonality	Atonal	Atonal	Atonal	Atonal	Atonal	Mixture
Texture	Pointillistic	Integrated	Synthesized	Dense polyphony	Neo–Romantic	Consolidated
Form	Closed	Closed	Closed	Closed	Closed	Closed
Instrumentation	Chamber forces	Large orchestra & percussion	Large orchestra & percussion	Large orchestra & percussion	Medium–size orchestra	Mixture of large & chamber
Extra Musical Considerations	Universal Theme (Metaphysical)	Universal Theme (Death at Hiroshima)	Universal Theme (Death at Golgotha, Auschwitz)	Universal Theme (Biblical)	Universal Theme (National, political, liturgical)	Universal Theme (Ethical values)

that produce a "sonoristic" musical style (1958–67); (3) [synthesis] the synthesis of this modern musical language with traditional stylistic elements (1962–72); (4) [sophistication] the phase of highly complicated experiments with vocal sonorities, dense polyphony and expressive melodic writing (1972–74); (5) [synchronization] the phase of blending the common elements of Penderecki's modern musical language into a more expressive style (1975–86); and (6) [stabilization] the consolidation of all the elements of his mature style into a more concise and personal musical language (1986–). These style phases are listed horizontally on the chart, while the musical elements are presented vertically on the left hand side of the chart.

PENDERECKI'S STYLE PERIODS

Using the factors discussed above as our primary evidence (the composer's ideas on style periods, the complications that the overlapping of style characteristics brings to the process, and Chart 1), the composer's musical pilgrimage can be organized into three macro periods: the period of search, the period of synthesis and the period of stability.

SEARCH

The period of search in Penderecki's music covers the years of the experimental works: 1956–67. Its primary characteristics include those that were discussed above in Phase 2: sonoristic musical language, controlled aleatorism, large orchestra with unusual instruments, free atonalism as a mode of linear expression, micro–tones, dense vertical cluster events, space–time notation, closed forms and universal–symbolic themes. The sonoristic works composed after 1962 cause significant overlapping in this category. We have sub–titled this period "the composer's time of exploration".

SYNTHESIS

The term synthesis has been used to define the next period in the composer's musical pilgrimage, 1962–1974. These are the years when Penderecki turns to tradition for his inspiration and consequently his work is marked by references to the past (liturgical texts, Renaissance and Baroque forms fugue, motet, passacaglia, thematic interpolations, the B–A–C–H motive, Polish hymn tunes, etc.). The inclination toward vocal writing, emphasis on large forms, and symbolic and universal themes such as death, intolerance, persecution, and evil all lead to a very direct artistic expression. These are works that carry a kind of double coding aesthetically: they are "modern" in the sense that they are based on the composer's unique musical language—sonorism, indeterminacy, serially–conceived linear events, vertical cluster "chords", space–time notation—but they transcend the limitations of the recognized avant–garde language of the period. "There is no denying their modernism, and yet they do not sound modern," to adopt a phrase coined by the *New York Times* critic Harold C. Schonberg on the occasion of the American première of the *St. Luke Passion.*[11] Would it be appropriate to call these works "Post–Modern?" This period could be subtitled "the melding of traditional elements with the composer's 'modern' musical language."

STABILITY

Stability is the term we will use to describe the most recent period in the composer's work: when his original musical language has been transformed into a very personal style (1975—). Certain elements of his "modern" language—free metric passages, sonorism, free atonality, linear events, clusters, closed formal models and symbolic references—continue as the basis of his compositional craft, but they are now part of a mature and stable musical expression, a new kind of "modernism", if you will. Penderecki is now writing *his* [emphasis mine] music; he is simply trying to compose "good" music for the audience he is reaching. In this late style period he has moved beyond the kind of synthesis, pluralism, or eclecticism that marked the second period works. There are, of course, still references to the past because Penderecki is continually inspired by tradition (*i.e.* the influence of the chamber music of Franz Schubert on his recent *Quartet for Clarinet and Strings)*. But today he feels very comfortable with his art. This period might be subtitled "the time of integrating certain 'modern elements' from his earlier period into his contemporary music language."

PENDERECKI'S MUSICAL SIGNATURES

Once we have surveyed the composer's works and investigated them for their style distinctives, we recognize that Penderecki is at least partially–correct when he states "that there is really only one style in my music." While there are major changes during the forty–year period of his career, there are, at the same time, many elements of his musical language that remain consistent throughout these years, thus giving weight to the argument that the connections with "modernism" which Penderecki seems particularly interested in preserving are those he has had a role in creating. It is helpful, we believe, to conclude this article with a short discussion of these so–called "Penderecki signatures". There are six such compositional elements that can be recognized consistently throughout the composer's works.

1. Sonority: the orchestra and voice are exploited for their coloristic qualities. In the early years the works are dominated by these compositional devices. Penderecki is more select in the use of these techniques in later works, but they appear in some form in nearly every composition. These

are the musical elements which make his works distinctive, his musical language very personal.

2. Various meter–tempo–rhythm devices: there is always at least one passage in every work where the composer suspends rhythm for the purpose of creating tension or release. Early in his career these devices were the "time graph" and "space–time" notation; later these are called "freely–rhythmic" passages.
3. Serialism and free atonality: from *Strophes* to the *Violin Concerto No. 2* the linear material developed is based on a freely atonal scale model. There are times, such as the second movement of the *Psalms of David* where Penderecki is writing "serial music"; there are others when he uses eight or nine units of the scale as the basis of constructing a freely atonal melodic line; but the source of the musical material is consistent throughout, as well as the predilection for the intervals of the minor second and tritone and the practice of octave displacement of the linear line as an extension of the range of the line within a phrase or passage.
4. Clustered vertical events: cluster "chords" with glissandi in their various forms are an ever–present signature of Penderecki's "harmonic" style in all phases of his compositional career. In the earlier works these horizontal events may take the form of dense micro–tonal clusters (*Polymorphia*); after 1962 they often appear as widely–spaced, open position 12–tone clusters (*Stabat mater*); and in recent works cluster technique is used very sparingly and primarily for the purpose of creating moments of "tension" and "release". A so–called "Penderecki signature chord"—consisting of a Major–minor chord with a tritone (or flatted–fifth degree of the scale) in the bass"—is used frequently in works like *Magnificat, Violin Concerto* No. 1, *Paradise Lost, Te Deum*, and "Sanctus" from the *Polish Requiem.*
5. Closed form: Penderecki has never had an inclination to leave the formal element of his style to chance.The structure of his works is always clear and logical. Where there is a text, the form generally follows the construction of the text. In one movement instrumental works, the form is usually based on the creation of tension and release.
6. Extra–musical considerations: the association of Penderecki's music with a humanistic or symbolic idea in the form of a social, national or universal theme is consistent in each style phase of the composer's work, from *Strophes* to *Ubu Rex*. But there seems to be less a tendency for this element to be present in his works after 1989. This makes one wonder whether the resolution of the political situation in Poland has had a subconscious liberating effect on the composer's art.

The very fact that these "common musical elements" appear in all phases and periods of the composer's work gives one cause to consider more seriously the composer's most recent thoughts on his stylistic development (i.e. "that there is really only one style period in my works"). Chart II illustrates this point.

Chart II
Musical Elements in Penderecki's Pilgrimage
Macro Form Chart

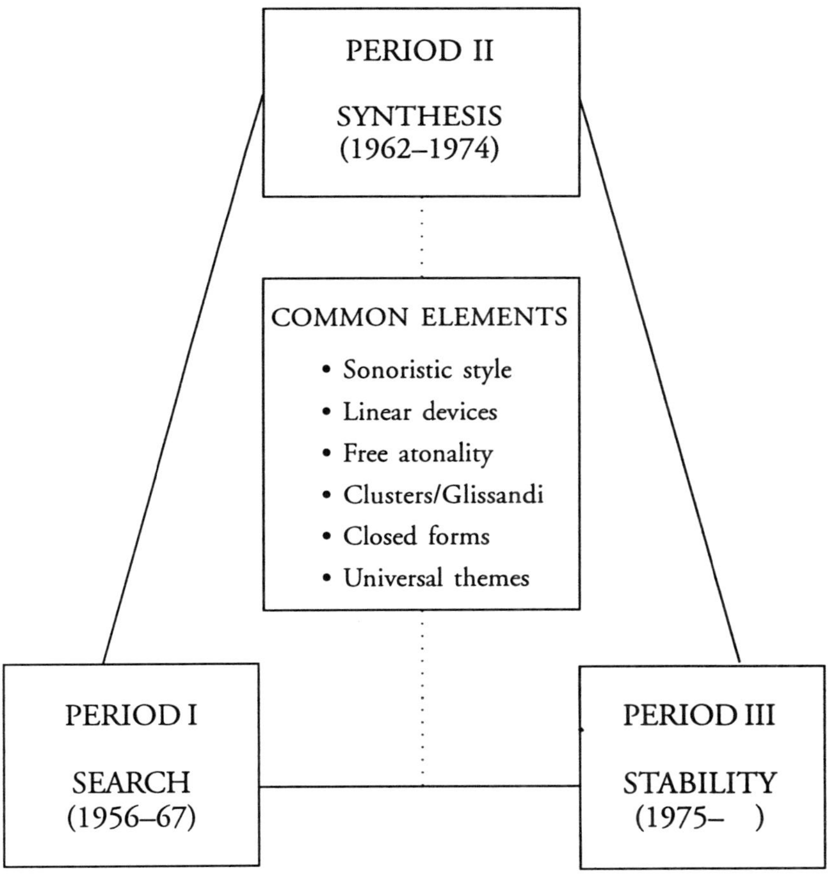

Conclusion

In a career that has now reached its fifth decade, Penderecki has consistently demonstrated an uncanny ability to compose music that is at once modern and timely. By choosing texts that speak in a prophetic way to the political and social issues of our time, he has met his audience at a point of humanistic communication. In composing works for events that relate to the history and plight of modern man he has established a relevance with his time that few other composers can match. The *St. Luke Passion* continues to be representative of this new quality he has brought to the music of the last half of the 20th century. It is a contemporary work that speaks very directly, and yet its eclectic musical language contains few of elements of the most intellectually "correct" stream of first half of the century (total serialism), and in the process rejects aspects of the sonoristic music in the instrumental and vocal innovations of his own hand. Penderecki's works today continue these two dimensions of his creativity: directness and modernity. Some criticize the composer for his desire to communicate so directly with his audience. This writer would agree with Erich Kahler "that no single event has artistic value unless it has generally human relevance. The true artist reaches beyond the phenomenal level. He drives into a depth of intensity where it is every human being's concern and potentiality."[12]

So it is with the musical pilgrimage of Krzysztof Penderecki. All stylistic tributaries lead to one main stream: the ability to speak at once in aesthetic and human terms with the passionate, sweeping vigor of truth. It is this balance between the frontier of the novel—conquering the hitherto untouched, ungrasped, unrevealed—and the unique ability to "reach" his audience through his original musical language that keeps Penderecki's art "contemporary".

NOTES

1. Quoted in: Krzysztof Penderecki, *Polish Music* 12:3 (1971), p. 25.

2. Quoted in: David Felder and Mark Schneider, "An Interview with Krzysztof Penderecki," *The Composer* 7 (1976–77), pp. 19–20.

3. Quoted in: Ray Robinson, "Krzysztof Penderecki: an Interview and Analysis of Stabat mater, *The Choral Journal* 24:3 (November 1983), p. 7.

4. Interview with the composer at his country home in Lusławice, Poland, July 14, 1993.

5. Quoted in: Krzysztof Droba, editor, *Festiwal Muzyki Krzysztofa Pendereckiego*: Kraków, Lusławice, Poznań, 9–16 VI 1988 (Kraków: June 1988, p. 7)

6. For a detailed musical analysis of the *Passion*, refer to: Ray Robinson and Allen Winold, *A Study of the Penderecki 'St. Luke Passion'* (Celle: Moeck Verlag, 1983). There is also a German edition available from the publisher.

7. Ray Robinson and Allen Winold, *op. cit.*, p. 6.

8. Teresa Malecka, editor, *Krakowska Szkoła Kompozytorska 1888–1988* (Kraków: Akademia Muzyczna, 1992), p. 333.

9. Quoted in Robinson, *op. cit.*, p. 8–9.

10. *Ibid*, p. 11.

11. Harold C. Schonberg, "Romanticism Coming Up?", *The New York Times*, March 16, 1969, Arts Section.

12. Erich Kahler, *The Disintegration of Form in the Arts*, (New York: George Braziller, 1968), p. 13.

Regina Chłopicka

CRACOW

Stylistic Phases in the Work of Krzysztof Penderecki

Krzysztof Penderecki's creative personality is a unique phenomenon in our time, both fascinating and disturbing. Full of dynamism and vitality, the passion to construct and transform, the composer imprints his mark on everything that he encounters on his way. At the time when a sense of inability, crisis or disorientation, numerous frustrations and even attempts to escape from the chaos of reality are so common in artistic circles, the composer who comes in affirming the sense of life and art and intensively experiencing the joy of existence seems to be an extraordinary character. The Renaissance versatility of interest — from the love of ancient culture, to expert knowledge of painting and architecture, the collector's passion for antique clocks, delight in cuisine, to the efforts to "tame the space" by designing the park and garden around his country house in Lusławice — this multiplicity of interests forms the climate in which musical ideas grow. In music Penderecki does not confine himself to composition. Already in the 1970's he took up conducting, which has since become his second nature. It has given him the opportunity to form the living musical matter, to give tangible shape to both his own works and those of other composers, to enact a clash between his own artistic personality and various groups of performers and audiences, to exert a suggestive, direct influence on people. His vigorous lifestyle, series of concert tours around the world alternating with periods of intensive creative work, could not fail to have influenced the composer's music.

PREPARATION YEARS

The stage which had preceded the creative years of Penderecki's life, a significant stage in terms of his personality development, was the period 1951–58. It is then that the future composer makes a choice as to his course of studies, tries to look around for his master and role models. These years are important as then certain characteristic patterns of the composer's personality begin to emerge, such as the wide spectrum of interests, independence, drive towards acquiring knowledge by himself, as well as a certain dynamism, a strength of character which has always allowed him to withstand the pressure of his environment.

The first musical experiences of the composer are piano lessons (discontinued after a short time), efforts to learn to play the violin on his own, as well as first composition attempts for the school music group, which do not go much beyond amateur activity, just as his first literary or painting efforts. In the 1960's, the composer described this period of his life in the following way:

> As a young man I was interested in painting and architecture, and that teaches one a lot about perspective and balance. Architecture in particular has said a good deal to me, and various concepts of architectural form and shape have been vital to my own thoughts about the structure of a work.[1]

His systematic musical education dates back to 1951, when Penderecki comes to stay in Cracow for a year, which ends with his choice of a study profile (humanities, string instruments, composition). He learns to play the violin (Stanisław Tawroszewicz) and studies music theory (Franciszek Skołyszewski); he also attends lectures in philosophy (Roman Ingarden) and classical philology (Tadeusz Sinko), trying to specify his areas of interest and, which is perhaps even more important, to assess realistically his own dispositions. At this stage of uncertainty and hesitation, which later led to Penderecki's ultimate choice of composition as the major field of study, the encounter with the original and passionately creative personality of Franciszek Skołyszewski was of particular significance. A mathematician and a physicist, a theorist of music and a pianist, a person of an extraordinarily broad mind, Skołyszewski was able to influence the young composer in two ways: on the one hand he inspired his imagination, and on the other, managed to impose on him the strict discipline in learning composition techniques, setting very high standards, especially in the area of counterpoint. From the perspective of many years, Penderecki saw his teacher in this way:

> I owe him my entire musical development, since it was him (*sic*) who discovered my talent and kept encouraging me.[2]

He seems to be the only person in Penderecki's training years who might be called his master. When a student in the State Higher School of Music in the composition class of Artur Malawski, and following his death, in the class of Stanisław Wiechowicz, Penderecki fulfills all requirements set by the school; and yet the process of development of his creative personality takes place mainly outside academia, then strongly neoclassical in its teaching methods. Penderecki searches for new models, he studies the works of Bartók, Stravinsky, Messiaen, and later comes across the scores of such composers as Nono, Webern and Boulez. The new models, however, are gradually rejected by Penderecki, although in his early works he does make references to them. And thus in the *Miniatures* for violin and piano one can find references to Webern's style, in

Psalms of David, to Stravinsky's rhythmical patterns, and in *Strophes*, to Nono's and Boulez's pointillistic technique. Penderecki has this to say about that period:

> Well up to the end of 1956 I went through a Bartók phase, and then when the restrictions were lifted I got to know other kinds of modern music. The Stravinsky of the *Symphony of Psalms* was important to me, and for a few months I was interested in Boulez, especially his *Mallarmé Improvisations*, but it did not last. Boulez and I really think quite differently.... As for the Darmstadt school, well we never had a real point of contact. In a way, I suppose, you could say that the difference between Darmstadt and me was that they were interested in dots, whereas I was interested in lines.[3]

CREATIVE DEVELOPMENT

The works of Krzysztof Penderecki vary very much with respect to genres, structures and types of expression, as well as composing techniques and sound material. His style transformation pattern, however, is marked primarily with oratorios/cantatas and stage works which take up grand themes. In order to produce a large–scale work, Penderecki creates a peculiar, internally cohesive musical language which constitutes its basic framework. The instrumental music, except in the composer's early period, is designed only to anticipate, complement or conclude the consecutive stages in his creative life. For many years it was an experimental field, a relaxation, or even a diversion for Penderecki, while he had the "serious" vocal–instrumental music on his mind. In instrumental, especially concerto music, the composer manifests his technical perfection in a given stylistic phase by writing virtuoso pieces, which allow the instrumentalists to experience the joy of their performance.

In the individual style of Krzysztof Penderecki two sets of features might be distinguished. The first comprises the features which are permanent or undergo only slight modifications and reflect the attitude of the composer towards formal aspects of music. Penderecki clearly prefers a closed form with a well–defined structure, the dramaturgy of which stems from a certain pattern of tension development, which can be achieved by different means. This is connected with a certain characteristic emphatic character, a certain clarity or even pathos of musical gesture. Its rhetorical nature has probably something to do with a peculiar, quasi–theatrical imagination of the composer. The second set of features which typify Penderecki's music contains features which, in the course of time, undergo clear transformations; they are due to the composer focusing his attention on different elements or layers of his work in different periods of time: on sound material, interval structures, polyphonic texture, melodic and harmonic structures, metro–rhythmic structures, etc. This in turn brings about, in consecutive phases of his work, a change in the hierarchy of elements of his musical language, leading to changes in style.

1958–1962
IN SEARCH OF INDIVIDUAL LANGUAGE
THE DRAMATIZED SONORISM
FROM *EMANATIONS* TO *FLUORESCENCES*

Penderecki starts his creative path from attempts to broaden and enrich sound material, the search for new techniques of its organization and experiments in notation. He expands the spectrum of instrumental (and then also vocal) tone colors to include a number of new hues, which are obtained mainly through unconventional methods of sound articulation, a peculiar treatment of sound pitch (smooth "waving" of pitch, quarter–tones and glissandos, cluster technique, etc.) and the incorporation of new sources of sound.[4] The composer employs various means of internal organization of sound segments—from free forms to those regulated by means of mathematical principles (applied primarily to sound groups and rhythms).[5] The multiplication of certain sound models or model families within a given segment leads to the development of the whole repertoire of textures, with tone–color coming to the forefront.[6] The contrasts between segments of varying texture constitute, in this period, the basis of a formal pattern, similar to an assembly form, although channeled in a special way. This type of development has been called by Nikolska "purposeful dramaturgy."[7] An integrated character of many pieces from that time is further strengthened by the way unisons are employed: they occur at significant moments as "texture X–rays" and create quasi tonal reference points, tonal centers of a kind. The pattern of their occurrence emphasizes the general formal plan of each work. Notational innovations concern on the one hand the way new sound effects are written down, and on the other, the time patterns of the works. The composer makes use mainly of different variants of proportional notation, specified further by metronomic indications or time measures expressed in seconds.[8] This phase of Penderecki's work is dominated by small instrumental pieces. The more important among them are: *Emanations* (1958), *Anáklasis* (1960), *Threnody to the Victims of Hiroshima* (1960), *Polymorphia* (1961) and *Fluorescences* (1962), and among vocal–instrumental pieces — *Psalms of David* (1958), *Strophes* (1959) and *Dimensions of Time and Silence* (1960).

1963–1974
IN SEARCH OF UNIVERSAL VALUES
BETWEEN SONORISM AND POLYPHONY—DRAMATURGY OF GRAND FORM
FROM THE *PASSION* TO *MAGNIFICAT*

The sphere of the musical avant–garde — sonorism, constructivism or serialism — even if it has enriched the composer's technical repertoire, ceases to suffice now. He abandons the avant–garde just as impetuously as he previously adopted it, and searches for his individual niche outside, without giving up what he has gained from the movement. He wants to write music that addresses people, he wants to be listened to and reacted to not only by the professionals. He searches for a universal theme which would unite people and evoke a response at all times, the theme which would transcend state frontiers and barriers of nationality, religious denomination, and culture. He finds it in the story of the passion and death of Jesus Christ. In 1965 Penderecki completes the *Passion According to St Luke*, and a few years later the two–part *Utrenya* (part I: *The Entombment of Christ*, part II: *The Resurrection*), thus producing a paschal tryptic. Aiming at universalism he does not play down the differences between Latin culture within which he grew up and Eastern Orthodox culture which fascinates him. He brings into play two distinct ways of thinking and expression in order to create two distinct visions of human attitude towards the world. The spiritual formation of Western Christianity, dominated by personalism, dynamic attitude to this world, and a clear balance between rationality and emotion form the basis of the *Passion According to St Luke.*

On the other hand, the characteristic breaking up with external reality, the emotional, often ecstatic nature of Eastern liturgy, which leads up to mystical experience, a peculiar type of contemplation, become an inspiration to create the musical world of *Utrenya.* Such a grand theme constituted a compositional challenge: it required a large vocal–instrumental form which would be internally cohesive and would have a certain architecture and dramaturgy. The starting point for the dramaturgy of the *Passion* was a text consisting of extracts from liturgical texts, which was designed by Penderecki to function as a script. In order to obtain powerful musical contrasts within one work, the composer employed, on the one hand, a number of techniques which were traditional (mainly Renaissance and Baroque) although transformed in a certain way, and on the other, several contemporary techniques. This resulted in the emergence of two contrasting worlds of sound; their opposition, co–occurrence or overlap form the basis of the musical dramaturgy of the *Passion* and the matching dramaturgy of its text. These worlds symbolize the spheres of contrasting values: good and evil, love and hatred, loyalty and betrayal. The sphere which symbolizes positive values is dominated by vocal forces, by thinking in terms of intervals and structure, by textures resulting from the employment of traditional, mainly polyphonic techniques, by slower tempos and heightened continuity of narration.

The sphere symbolizing negative values, on the other hand, is often dominated by instrumental forces, by the sonoristic treatment of sound material, by multiple illustrative effects, by contrastiveness, nonlinearity and unevenness of sequencing as well as by the accelerated narrative pace. The internal cohesion of the work is achieved first by the integration of sound material — the work is based on two twelve–tone series of a characteristic structure (domination of the interval cell containing a semi–tone and a minor third, symmetry of interval patterns, etc.) — and second, by a system of anticipation and repetition of words and motives of symbolic significance (from the BACH motive, included in the series, to the frequently recurring "Domine" motive).[9] The integration of the form is further enhanced by the overall plan of tonal references (G,D,A,E); the closing of the work on the full, pure E major triad and the words *"Deus Veritatis"* may be interpreted not only as a logical solution to the musical sequence, but also as a more general, symbolic message: the message of hope. In the two–part *Utrenya*, written a few years later, the vocal and orchestral forces are expanded even more and the further development of polyphonic techniques takes place. The elaborate polyphonic structures, although usually inaudible, become the internal organizing principle of the sound layer. Aside from linear polyphony, we can also observe here the polyphony of sound segments, bundles or bands, which leads to the emergence of a monumental and colourful "sound fresco"; this combines the ecstatic atmosphere of Orthodox liturgy with the hieratic, symbolic vision of the icon.[10] It is in *Magnificat* that the polyphonic structuring reaches its climactic point; there the polyphony of sound layers constitutes the structural basis of the double–theme fugue (*Quia respexit*).[11] Simultaneously, *Magnificat* (as well as the *Awakening of Jacob*) brings an early signal of another coming stylistic transformation: the initial chord exhibits a special harmonic function (a minor–major chord with the lowered fifth in the bass). This kind of treatment of harmonic structure anticipates the return to the dominating position of melodic–harmonic structures and techniques of their processing, which is characteristic of the next phase of Penderecki's work. The most important works of the present phase, apart from *The Passion*, *Utrenya* and *Magnificat* (1974), are the *Dies Irae* oratorio (1967), *The Devils of Loudun* opera (1969) and *Cosmogony* (1970), and in the field of instrumental music — *De natura sonoris* I and II (1966 and 1970–1) and *Symphony No. 1* (1973).

1974–1980
IN SEARCH OF MUSIC'S PARADISE LOST
THE SPHERE OF NEO–ROMANTICISM
FROM *PARADISE LOST* TO *SYMPHONY No. 2*

In the third phase of Penderecki's work the expressive melodic line, linked to a certain harmony, emerges as the focus of the composer's interest, while the contrasting harmonic structures form the starting point for the dramaturgy of the pieces then written. *In Paradise Lost*, three harmonic features: the octave, the third–based chord from *Magnificat* and the twelve–tone tritone–second chord constitute the basic sound structures which characterise God, man and Satan, respectively.[12] The emotionally tense type of expression, which is a reference to neo–Romanticism, is obtained by the domination of melodic–harmonic structures, the introduction of the development techniques which characterize musical narration, as well as the conscious return to the instrumentation based on Rimsky–Korsakov's "certainty of harmony" principle, as the composer himself put it before the work was finished. Both the structural, interval–based techniques and sonoristic techniques, as well as linear structures are gradually marginalized. The monumental dimensions and the dramatic and poetic character of Milton's epic find a rather unusual reflection in Penderecki's work.

His *Paradise Lost* is a mystery–like piece, a grand "fresco" which goes back to the Baroque *sacra rappresentazione* tradition where the monumental vocal and instrumental forces served to illustrate the Biblical story of salvation. The consecutive dramatically expressive stages of the story — the drama of fallen angels, the creation of the world and man, the rebellion of Satan against God leading to the sin and fall of man, the saving sacrifice of Christ, and finally, the grand vision of the Apocalypse — all symbolically point to the clash of the forces of good and evil. Just as in the *Passion*, musical dramaturgy is based on the fundamental contrast between the world of sound which represents good and the world of evil. Still, in *Paradise Lost* these two worlds of sound (created with different musical means than in the previous phase) constitute two opposing poles and two reference points for the third world — the world of man; man and his consecutive transformations effected under the influence of the opposing forces of good and evil, God and Satan, become the central theme of the work. The grand final scene of the imminent future Apocalypse takes place in front of Adam. The scene is a *passacaglia*, the theme of which is a quotation from the medieval *Dies irae* sequence, traditionally a symbol of fear and annihilation. This is not the only quotation introduced by the composer in *Paradise Lost*. The scene in which Christ sacrifices his life for man culminates with the quotation from Bach's chorale.

The employment of quotations, which in the course of Penderecki's work becomes more and more frequent, seems to be one of the ways of stressing the continuity of cultural tradition, a dialogue with the past. Symphony No 2, dominated by the harmony of thirds and development technique, shows an even closer link with the neo–Romantic symphonic style, particularly in the language. The way themes are contrasted and developed, leading to dramatic culminations, is a reference to the sonata tradition in its neo–Romantic phase. The piece, also called "Christmas Symphony", includes a quotation of the "Silent Night" Christmas carol. Another important piece from this period is *Concerto No. 1* for violin (1976–77), which is very closely related to *Paradise Lost.*

1980–1984
IN SEARCH OF A NATIONAL IDENTITY
GRAND SYMPHONIC STYLE AND LITURGICAL TRADITION
FROM *TE DEUM* TO THE *POLISH REQUIEM*

In Penderecki's work the period starting from *Te Deum* and ending with the *Polish Requiem* is largely a continuation of the musical language developed in the previous phase. Nevertheless, certain new and important elements do appear then in his music. On the one hand, very intensive expression is curbed through reference to liturgical tradition, and on the other, the universal message carried by a series of works becomes marked with a new perspective: the composer's growing awareness of the close bond with the place on the earth he can call his own. The events important for Poland come to exert a stronger and stronger (and not only external) impact on his music. In 1980 Penderecki completes *Te Deum*, a solemn piece which in its very middle contains a passage from the Polish religious and patriotic anthem, *Boże coś Polske.* This reference to the Polish tradition has to do with the event which was to have great influence on the subsequent history of Poland: the election of Cardinal Karol Wojtyła as Pope. In the same year, at the request of Lech Wałęsa, Penderecki writes a lamentation, *Lacrimosa*, to be performed at the unveiling ceremony of the Monument to the Victims of December 1970 in Gdańsk, the embodiment of national rebellion against Communist oppression. Together with *Agnus Dei*, written in 1981, for the funeral of the uncompromising Primate of Poland, Cardinal Stefan Wyszyński (kept in prison by the Communist authorities in the 1950's), *Lacrimosa* has formed the core of the Polish Requiem. The work is based on the Latin *missa pro defunctis* texts, although the central section of the *Dies irae* sequence (another movement of the *Polish Requiem*, a passacaglia), contains a quotation from the *Święty Boże* supplication prayer sung in Poland in moments of national danger. It appears in counterpoint to the Latin "Recordare Jesu pie" text and plays the role of a theme of Dies irae. Both this quotation and the dedications of the other movements, which are related to tragic historical experiences the Poles went through during World War II — the massacre of Katyń, the death camp of Oświęcim [Auschwitz] and the defeat of Warsaw Uprising — clearly illustrate the composer's attitude to the history of his nation, especially that the *Polish Requiem* came into being at the time when Poland was under another threat: the martial law. In the *Polish Requiem* the composer, while retaining the dramatism of form, its monumental dimensions and the pathos of musical gestures, restrains and rationalizes the expression of melodic–harmonic structures in the spirit of Latin liturgy, thus returning in a sense to the oratorio style of the *Passion According to St Luke*. At the same time, however, due to the distinctiveness of language and techniques employed, the development and integration of musical form take place organically, as if within music. Its logic does not stem from the textual script, although the links with the text are obviously present. The symphonic type of thinking dominates. This phase of Penderecki's work brings a synthesis of many previous experiences which leads to the state of a certain balance with respect to musical means.[13]

1984–1986

IN SEARCH OF LIMITS OF EXPRESSION
DANSE MACABRE IN EXPRESSIONISTIC THEATRE
DRAMATURGY OF ACCELERATION
THE WORLD OF THE *BLACK MASK*

At this stage it is for the third time after *The Devils of Loudun* and *Paradise Lost* that Penderecki turns to musical theatre. Fascinated with the art of Gerhard Hauptmann, he writes the expressionistic *Black Mask* opera. The theme of death, which keeps returning in the composer's works, reaches its climax here. The *Black Mask* is an extended theatrical scene which depicts the situation before the imminently approaching catastrophe, the situation involving a tangled–up matrix of exaggerated emotions. Exclusively for the sake of this work, the composer creates an individual musical language, within which musical narration becomes dominated by movement and rhythm.

Dynamic sequences of changeable meters predominate, while sharp accents and rich motion patterns give the impression of continuous feverish acceleration. Rhythmical patterns are full of contrasts, from full ordering, an almost march–like character, to ad libitum sections where free repetition of quick figurative phrases is often regulated by intricate counterpoint. Tensions obtained in that way are further strengthened by sharp seconds–fifths harmonies and textural contrasts, as well as characteristic means employed in orchestral parts (tremolos, trills, quick repetitions, etc.) and lead to subsequent fierce culminations, which results in the emergence of a characteristic "dramaturgy of acceleration." In the structure of the opera an important role is played by quotations; excerpts from 17th century dance music or Protestant choral as well as self–

quotations (the opera contains the passages from *Te Deum* and the *Polish Requiem*), alongside with the division of musical space into multiple planes, all enhance dramatic contrasts. *The Black Mask* is one of the few works by Penderecki which end in a symbolic catastrophe. The characters are led in a symbolic dance of death towards annihilation. The only character that remains is Perl, a witness, the symbolic figure of a Wandering Jew. Technical means, type of expression and dramaturgy clearly link the *Black Mask* to the tradition of expressionistic theatre, and even though in the earlier work of the composer one can find anticipatory signals of such style (e.g. the exorcisms scene in the *Devils of Loudun*), it reaches its maximum intensity only in the *Black Mask*.[14]

1987–1992
IN SEARCH OF NEW AREAS OF EXPERIENCE
FROM THE CLASSICAL "PLAY CONVENTION" TO THE PLAY OF CONVENTIONS IN POST—MODERNIST THEATRE
BETWEEN *SINFONIETTA* AND *UBU REX*

In this phase of his work, Krzysztof Penderecki focuses his interest on two areas: the further development of instrumental concert music genres (new versions of *Concerto for Viola*, *Concerto for Flute* (1992), *Sinfonietta per archi* (1992), and the search for new areas of theatrical experience. The first group of works includes *Sinfonietta per archi*, in which instrumental lyricism and the dramatized scherzo character are expressed in a nearly neoclassical form. Sinfonietta is an orchestral version of the earlier String Trio. Its first movement is a reference to the tradition of baroque concertos in the ritornello form, in which the full orchestra passages are separated by solo instrumental parts. The second movement (from the structural point of view) combines elements of a sonata allegro with a scherzo–type form, which contains two trio sections. The musical material of the work has been signficantly influenced by an instrumental passage from *Ubu Rex*.

The new experiences in theatre work were encapsulated in the *Ubu Rex* comic opera, completed in 1991, based on the text by Alfred Jarry. The Ubu King of the title is a puppet–like monster, the embodiment of the destructive, cruel and dull power of stupidity, which at the moment of danger, however, shows cowardice and weakness. This highly archetypical character might appear under a new disguise at any time or place. The musical interpretation of Jarry's proposed by Penderecki brings into the foreground the comical character and grotesque features of the character, partly playing down his aggressiveness and vulgarity apparent in the language and stage situations. The *Ubu Rex* opera has challenged Penderecki with new problems: the problem of the distinctiveness of the comic opera genre and the dividing line between the serious and the buffo convention, as well as the problem of finding the musical equivalent for the joke, mockery, the comical and the grotesque contained in Jarry's play. In his opera, Penderecki makes references on the one hand to the musical tradition of *opera buffa* (Pergolesi and Hasse, Mozart and Rossini) and musical drama (Wagner and Strauss), and on the other, to experiences of 20th century theatre—Artaud's cruelty theater, Beckett's, Ionesco's or Mrożek's theatre of the absurd and grotesque drama—which makes the events of the work strongly ambiguous.

In the music of the opera, the composer keeps oscillating around the borderline between the serious and the buffo, surprising us with allusive, out–of–the–context references to conventions. The whole catalogue of comic effects in the opera could be compiled, based on the choice of material, types of motives, quotations or references, to familiar musical genres (the waltz, polonaise, march). In the dramaturgy of the opera, tensions are usually achieved through situations of surprise, through clashes between incompatible musical conventions, which are exaggerated and their features overstated. In this game of conventions a serious musical phrase and a solemn Wagnerian gesture may appear side by side with a trivial text and suddenly close with a banal cadence, showing its grotesque face to us: a virtuoso "serious" cadence turns out to be an absurd joke.

Krzysztof Penderecki's *Ubu Rex* opera, however, is not only play. Through the comical, caricature and the grotesque the composer conveys the idea of a threat posed to man by the world of absurd, cruel play, in which all values have been rejected.[15]

1992—?
IN SEARCH OF CLASSICAL BEAUTY IN THE SPHERE OF "NEW LYRICISM" FROM *QUARTET FOR CLARINET* TO *CONCERTO NO. 2* FOR VIOLIN

The recent years in Penderecki's work have been characterized by the domination of instrumental music. He has spent a great deal of time working on symphonic pieces: the "Korean" *Symphony No. 5*, written in 1992, and *Symphony No. 3*, completed in 1995, two movements of which, *Passacaglia and Rondo*, came into being already in 1988. Interestingly, these recent pieces have a certain new ring to them.

In the hitherto work of Krzysztof Penderecki, from the *Passion* to the *Devils of Loudun* to the *Black Mask*, the sphere of darkness, dread and evil has been his constant fascination. Hence the inevitable domination of strongly contrastive, tense dramaturgy, rhetorical gestures and large–scale vocal–instrumental pieces with a message. If there were moments of lightening up and contemplation, they had to do merely with the symbolic longing for another reality, they were a sign of hope rather than its fulfilment. Now, from *Sanctus* (the movement which completes the *Polish Requiem*, written in 1992) to *Concerto for Flute* to *Concerto No. 2 for Violin*, the center of gravity seems to be gradually moving to the sphere of light and pure, classical beauty. We can observe a considerable reduction of musical means, a certain balance and classical proportions in the form, an overall quietening and a personal, almost intimate, lyrical tone. This is most apparent in the *Quartet for Clarinet and Strings*, written in 1993: listening to it one cannot help reflecting that, after many journeys, adventures and storms, the composer has eventually returned to his "native Ithaca."

Notes

1. Antes Orga, "Krzysztof Penderecki," *Music and Musicians* 22: 10 (October 1973), p. 40.

2. Tadeusz A. Zieliński, "Współczesny kompozytor a tradycja. Rozmowa z Krzysztofem Pendereckim," *Ruch Muzyczny* 12 (1963), p. 8–9.

3. Antes Orga, "Krzysztof Penderecki," *op. cit.*, p. 39.

4. See Tadeusz A. Zieliński, "Der einsame Weg der Krzysztof Penderecki, *Melos 29* (1962), p. 11; T.A. Zieliński, "Technika operowania instrumentami smyczkowymi w utworach Krzyszatofa Pendereckiego," *Muzyka (1968), p. 77–92;* T. Nordwall, "Krzysztof Penderecki. Studium notacji i instrumentacji," *Res Facta* (1968), p. 79–112; Wolfram Schwinger, *Penderecki: Begegnungen, Lebensdaten, Werkkommentare* (Stuttgart: Deutsche Verlagsanstalt, 1979); B. Malecka–Contamin, "Penderecki: Style et Materiaux (Thése de doctorat d'état, Université Paris, 1996).

5. Krzysztof Bilica, "Quartetto per archi (No. 1) Krzysztofa Pendereckiego" In: *Kwartet smyczkowy w polskiej muzyce współczesnej* (Kraków: Akademia Muzyczna, 1977), p. 85–95.

6. The mechanism according to which colorful segments come into being and their role in the shaping of form are discussed by Krzysztof Droba in: "Hierarchia czynników formalnych w twórczości Krzysztofa Pendereckiego," *Muzyka* (1976), no. 2, p. 22–28. See also Willi Gruhn, "Strukturen und Klangmodelle in Penderecki's Threnos'", *Melos* (1971) Heft 10.

7. Irina Nikolska, "On Some Symphonic Works within the 80s" In: *The Music of Krzysztof Penderecki, Poetics and Reception* (Kraków: Akademia Muzyczna, 1995), p. 51.

8. T. Nordwall, *op. cit*, p. 79–112.

9. Brunhilde Kaack, "Pendereckis Zwölftonreihe," *Musica* 29:1 (1975); Manfred Schuler, "Tonale Phänomene in Pendereckis 'Lukas–Passion'", Melos/NZ 1 (January–February 1976), p. 457–460; Wolfram Schwinger, *Penderecki*, p. 202–220.

10. Regina Chłopicka, "Związki z liturgią prawosławną w Jutrzni Krzysztofa

Pendereckiego" In: *Księga jubileuszowa Mieczysława Tomaszewskiego* (Kraków, Akademia Muzyczna, 1984), p. 119–139.

11. Regina Chłopicka, "Technika polifoniczna w Magnificat. Słowo i dżwięk w 'Magnificat' In: *Współczesność i tradycja w muzyce Krzysztofa Pendereckiego* (Kraków: Akademia Muzyczna, 1983), p. 187–205.

12. Regina Chłopicka, "Le Paradis perdu—sacra rappresentatione de Krzysztof Penderecki" In: *Problèmes, interferences des genres au théâtre et les fêtes en Europe* (Paris: Presses Universitaires de France, 1985): Joanna Wnuk–Nazarowa, "Postać szatana w Raju Utraconym" In: *Współczesność i tradycja w muzyce Krzysztofa Pendereckiego* (Kraków: Akademia Muzyczna, 1983), p. 221–232.

13. Andrzej Chłopecki, "Tryptyk paschalny" In: *Festiwal muzyki Krzysztofa Pendereckiego* (Kraków, 1988), p. 39–42; Regina Chłopicka, "Polish Requiem" In: *The Music of Krzysztorf Penderecki. Poetics and Reception* (Kraków: Akademia Muzyczna, 1995), p. 29–44; Mieczysław Tomaszewski, "Das Wort–Ton–Verhältnis bei Krzysztof Penderecki" In: *Zum Verhältnis von zeitgenössischer Musik und zeitgenössischer Dichtung* (Wien–Graz: Universal Edition, 1988).

14. Regina Chłopicka, "Le Masque noire de Krzysztof Penderecki" In: *Les premiers opéras en Europe et les formes dramatiques apparentées* (Paris: Klincksieck, 1992); Wolfram Schwinger, "Schwarze Maske im Kontext seiner szenischen Musik" In: *The Music of Krzysztof Penderecki, op. cit.*, p. 19–20.

15. Andrzej Chłopecki, "In a Hall of Mirrors or Ubu in Penderecki's Opera" In: *The Music of Krzysztof Penderecki, op. cit.*, p. 21–28.

Translated by Władysław Grzegorz Chłopicki

Wolfram Schwinger

STUTTGART

Changes in Four Decades: The Stylistic Paths of Krzysztof Penderecki

There is hardly another prominent composer of the second half of the twentieth century who has changed his style as often as Krzysztof Penderecki. He himself likes to cite his spiritual kinship with Pablo Picasso, who was always searching, always beginning anew. When others sought to imitate this great painter, he himself had already moved ahead to work in a new style.

Penderecki could just as well have mentioned other composers from the first half of the twentieth century, whose life work was marked by surprising changes of style. Stravinsky moved from Russian Impressionism and Expressionism to Neo–Classicism and, at the end of his life, to advanced serialism; Hindemith followed the opposite path from provocative objectivity [*Sachlichkeit*] to conservative traditionalism. Belá Bartók's stylistic evolution was marked not so much by contrasts, but rather by continuous development.

Penderecki's stylistic phases did not follow the successive development of Stravinsky or Hindemith, but they also did not follow the continuous development of Bartók. Instead he has made abrupt changes at two points in his stylistic development—first from the *Preludes* of his student years to the noise explosions [*Geräuschexplosionen*] of his early works and then from the decade of consolidation to a retrospective, markedly Romantic phase. Thereafter, in 1982 he begins a period of synthesis that extends to the present day in a process of continuous growth.

Preludes

In 1951, after Penderecki had concluded his schooling in his home town Dębica with the high school diploma, he went to Cracow to study music. He completed in two years the prescribed five–year music middle school program, which prepared students for advanced academic studies. Violin performance was his major. In 1954 he was accepted into the Academy of Music, where he studied for four years. He gave up his violin studies after two semesters, because he was determined to become a composer. His most important teacher at this time was Artur Malawski, one of the most eminent Polish composers after Szymanowski, a musician in the neo–romantic tradition with a preference for modern techniques such as polyrhythms. After his teacher's early death in 1957 Penderecki spent a year in the composition class of Stanisław Wiechowicz, who was successful above all in his choral music, in which he used strict instrumental forms and combined folkloristic elements with a richly differentiated harmonic language. In 1958 Penderecki finished his studies with such brilliance that the Academy awarded him not only a diploma, but also a teaching contract. Fourteen years later Penderecki would be appointed Rector of the same institution. Even before he began his academic studies, Penderecki in 1953 had composed a short three–movement *Sonata for Violin and Piano*. This work is astonishingly skillful in its musical craftmanship and rich in its musical ideas. Its first movement shows the influence of Prokofiev and Hindemith, especially in the way the musical materials are worked out. The middle movement, an elegiac *Andante*, pays homage in a sensitive manner to Bartók, not only in its major–minor mixture, but also in its melodic writing and in the arabesque–like spinning–out [*Fortspinnung*] of the thematic ideas and the use of changing meters (5/8, 4/8, 3/8, 6/8). The highly developed feeling for tone color and the skill in contrasting and combining the two instruments in this movement as well as in the finale are astonishing for a twenty–year–old composer. This entry into the field of composition was followed in the next year by the "Caprices for Solo Violin", that still remains unpublished.

The elegant *Miniatures* for clarinet and piano (1956) reveal in their harmonic and rhythmic aspects Penderecki's predilection at that time for Bartók. At the end of his academic studies, Penderecki, moved by the death of his teacher, composed his first larger work: *Epitaphium Artur Malawski in memoriam*, a two–movement instrumental requiem for string orchestra and timpani. It is his diploma composition, and already shows clear signs of his later writing, for example, in the solo viola passage with its minor second sigh–motives which introduce the meditative first movement, or in the glissandi of the development section, as well as in the chains of trills in the divided cellos that emerge in the second movement. The passionate expressivity of this music, as well as certain stylistic characteristics, could be traced to his knowledge of Arthur Honegger's *String Symphony* of 1941.

In 1959 Penderecki achieves a breakthrough to an ever stronger individual profile with three works, which earn him all three prizes of the composition competition of the Polish Association of Composers. The three works are *Psalms of David* for mixed chorus, stringed instruments and percussion; *Emanations* for two string orchestras; and *Strophes* for soprano, speaker, and ten instruments.

Penderecki was able to begin his compositional career in fortunate circumstances. Three years before the composition of these three works, at the time of the political revolution in Poland and the dethroning of Stalinismus, the regimentation of the arts was abrogated. Therefore, social realism was no longer prescribed for new music. Contacts with the latest musical developments in the West, which until then did not exist openly, could now be established without fear of punishment. For older composers such as Witold Lutosławski or Kazimierz Serocki this necessitated a strong re–orientation. The works that resulted from this change attained an important position from this time on at the music festivals of the Warsaw Autumn next to the compositions of Western exponents of the avant–garde—for example, in 1958 next to works of Stockhausen, Boulez, and Cage. Penderecki, by contrast, can begin unencumbered. He does not travel to the summer courses in Darmstadt, the center of the Western avant–garde at that time. However, he does not shut himself off from the new scores, that are now easy to obtain. His three prize–winning works of 1959 prove this clearly.

In his composition *The Psalms of David* it is possible to discern the inspiration of two great twentieth–century musical elders: Stravinsky in rhythmic and chordal elements of the first and third movements, and Schönberg in linear and structural characteristics of the second and fourth movements. With the adaptation of models such as these Penderecki already develops his own personal style characteristics, which he will expand and deepen in future compositions. In the first movement, for example, the five opening instrumental measures create a sound mass [*Geräuschfeld*], a rhythmically overlapping aural network of soft, tremolo percussion instruments. This anticipates an effect that will be the defining element in *Anáklasis*, the first successful work of the following year. The chorus sometimes sings and sometimes speaks on specified pitches, as in Schönberg's *Pierrot lunaire*. Chromatic quarter–tone clusters form layers of sound which can be designated as typically Pendereckian, even at this early date. Another similar sound surface is formed by the four timpani and four tom–toms which prepare for the double chorus in the second section of the first movement. The linear poetry of the second movement, an a cappella chorale, can be traced not only to the tradition of Gregorian chant, but also to the dodecaphony of Schönberg. It is also saturated with elements of traditional fugal technique. The third movement is a rhythmically explosive piece that is based on the vigorous ostinato technique of the neo–classic Stravinsky—somewhat in the same manner that the choral works of Carl Orff are based on Stravinsky's *Les Noces*. The chorus is assigned motoric repetitions, chordal blocks are saturated with linear motives, and syllables of the text are distributed among the various voices, a technique Penderecki frequently uses in later works. In the fourth movement Penderecki again employs the twelve–tone technique of the second movement, this time not a cappella, but with the support of instruments.

Emanations, with its sensitive timbral shading, tonal pointillism and predilection for wide intervals, certainly points to Penderecki's preoccupation with post–Webern serialism. However, to a large extent the sound of the work is already defined by his own personal timbral flow, which is characterized by long, drawn–out layers of sound differing greatly in intensity and prominence. This technique, relatively easy to grasp in this work, points clearly toward the more amorphous works of the following year. This short piece requires two string orchestras with the largest possible number of players. The instruments of the second orchestra must be tuned a minor second higher. This scordatura itself achieves the desired diffusion, a timbral mixture that is also frequently intensified through prescribed pitch alterations of a third–tone. These sounds flow in and out of one another (as signified in the title), and they are further differentiated through performance indications such as rapid, arhythmic tremolo, bowing near the fingerboard (*flautando*) or bridge (*sul ponticello*), and bowing or striking the strings with the wood of the bow (*col legno, col legno battuto*). Frequent harmonics or glissandi, playing with mutes or without vibrato, trills with strong finger attacks, and uncoordinated changes of bow are found in the score, as well as, at the very end, tremolo on open strings and glissandi produced by turning the tuning pegs.

With *Strophes* Penderecki draws his models from much younger composers. The atmosphere of this work would be unthinkable without the music of Luigi Nono, whom Penderecki met in 1958 when Nono visited Cracow. It would also be impossible to imagine these works without the inspiration of the works of Pierre Boulez, for example the poetry of his instrumental and vocal timbral amalgamation in *Marteau sans maître*, or the highly refined tonal sensualism of *Improvisations sur Mallarmé*, which Boulez himself characterized as a synthesis of Webern and late–Debussy. Both Penderecki and Boulez at that time prescribed fluctuating tempi from measure to measure and employed the noticeably soft colors of the xylophone, which contributed significantly to the instrumental and vocal timbral melding. Of course, the simultaneous use of *Sprechstimme* and singing refers obviously to Schönberg's *Moses and Aaron*. More important than such references is the fact that in *Strophes* one can recognize clearly the young Penderecki's individual style, which was emerging ever more clearly at this time, especially in the differentiated shading of his timbral coloring. Also the newly composed *Miniatures for Violin and Piano*, with their rapidly changing dynamic contrasts and their large intervallic leaps, point in two directions. On the one hand, they represent a farewell to the Webern world of thought, and on the other hand, they mark a stylistic departure in Penderecki's own sound world. This departure consists of a refined mixture of unusual performance indications and articulations (described above in connection with *Emanations*), which now become a characteristic of his musical handwriting. Everything is still notated in traditional music notation. In the future this will no longer suffice. For now, after these prize–winning works, Penderecki steps out of the preliminary stage of his creative efforts on to the main stage of his experimental endeavors, in which he will open up wholly new worlds of sound and expression for contemporary music.

Explosions

All of Penderecki's initiatives in the development of a new and personal style were somehow still linked to tradition. Immediately after the three compositions described above he finds the courage to break with tradition, to renounce completely all that he learned in his academic studies. At the same time, these works that originated in 1959–1960 represent violent opposition to dogmatic serial music, which was in the final stages of decay.

What he now developed may be categorized summarily with concepts such as *Klangfarbenmusik* [tone–color music] or *Klangflächenmusik* [sound–mass music or tonal–surface music]. Various composers at this point, notably Penderecki, Friedrich Cerha and György Ligeti, arrive at nearly identical results. They differ essentially in the structuring of the sound–masses. Penderecki creates his sound–masses primarily from tone clusters (for vertical density) and glissandi (for horizontal density); Cerha, on the other hand, develops massive structures through, so to speak, organic processes; while Ligeti patches together his clusters from micro–polyphonic network structures. He renounces Penderecki's global notation (as Ligeti called it). That is to say, he does not use black beams in a fascinating optical way to create a new image in his scores; instead he writes out his clusters note for note, because he wants to maintain control over the individual voice leading.

In the case of Penderecki, we can also find a micro–organic inner life, as proven by the extremely fastidious microrhythmic writing which appeared immediately in the first work in this new direction—in the middle section of *Anáklasis* for strings and percussion groups. Here quarter notes are divided into groups of four, five and six eighth notes, with interspersed rests. These groups overlap each other at various time intervals so as to create the desired dense sound–mass.

Moreover, it is a work of highly complex sound–effect structure in which the two highly varied instrumental groups are used for processes of assimilation. The meaning of the title *Anáklasis*, refraction of light, is used here in a figurative sense to connote refraction of sound colors, tonal dispersion and reassembly in subtle dynamic shadings. Penderecki is principally interested in the seamless change of sound characteristics, flexible transitions from sound to noise or vice versa from noise to sound, in other words in moving from hardness and dryness to various gradations of softness. The specific sound of the string and percussion instruments is so alienated and the function of the instruments is so radically changed that it almost seems as if one instrumental group assumes the sounding characteristics of the other. The composer thus demonstrates his skill in varying his cluster technique as well as his richly diverse spectrum of the most multifarious kinds of articulation or performance techniques on both string and percussion instruments. Penderecki invented many new symbols for the notation of these techniques. The three–part form of the composition corresponds to its sounding idea—thesis, antithesis, and synthesis. There are especially interesting periods of transition or reciprocal attempts at adaptation between the strings and percussion and between massive sound events and pointillistic sound events.

Another work from this period of frenzied compositional activity is *Dimensions of Time and Silence*, an equally important documentation of his investigation of musical materials at this time. To the string and percussion instruments Penderecki adds a forty–voice mixed chorus, that does not sing text but only phonemes. It is used in an almost instrumental manner as a producer of sounds and noises, which are sometimes poetic and sometimes an aggressive spectrum of consonants and vowels. The length of the individual sections is prescribed in seconds. The sections have strictly structured sound characteristics, which are presented, inverted, and combined. The consonant row GTKBDGPKD, for example, appears not only in retrograde DKPGDBKTG, but also as a combination of original and retrograde. A 12–tone vowel–row such as OYIAEUOIYEAU is woven at various points into the consonant structure. Penderecki shows his refined sense of color in this work as in *Anáklasis.* and gives the chorus a wide range of material ranging from noise–like, sharp consonants to soft sounds, and also including the musical use of vowels as pedal tones, and the use of breathy sounds, such as the rolled "R", the French "J", and the voiced "Sch." In the synthesis of the final sections the chorus sings clusters with various types of vibrato, sometimes whistled, sometimes in falsetto, with closed or open mouth. Then there are mixtures of percussion, chorus, and strings in highly varied articulations and dynamic levels.

In 1960 to 1961 Penderecki writes three works for strings alone in which (of all things, with these instruments) he carries his use of noise explosively and rabidly to the pinnacle of excess. The emotionally charged expressive energies of *Threnody* (for 52 string instruments) with its sharp pungency and often enervating noisiness could easily be interpreted as a naturalistic depiction of chaos. Beyond this, however, the densely woven study of the sound of Hiroshima has the power of a screaming lament and accusation, and it was this that encouraged Penderecki to dedicate it later to the first victims of the atom bomb.

In the exposition of this clearly sectionalized and flexibly constructed work the simplest sound types are juxtaposed. The first characteristic sound type involves irregular entrances of each instrument playing *fortissimo* strokes on their respective highest (unspecified) pitch. These are played with various types of vibrato—strong, slow, or in quarter–tones. The section lasts 50 seconds in the published score, 100 seconds in Penderecki's own recording. The second characteristic sound type involves aleatorically structured percussion effects by the strings. Each of the 52 players can choose one of four prescribed groupings which he or she then repeats as fast as possible within a specified period of time. The effects could include playing the highest note with rapid arhythmic tremolo, playing arpeggio *col legno* across the four strings between the bridge and the tailpiece, playing the highest note pizzicato, playing a single note between the bridge and the tailpiece, pounding with a finger or with the frog of the bow on the belly of the instrument, etc. These small groups of played sounds or percussive effects are indicated with special signs developed by Penderecki. They produce in ever–changing combinations a complex kaleidoscope of tone color that borders on noise. Similar aleatoric repetitions of structure may be found a short time later in 1961 in Lutosławski's *Jeux Venetiens.* Finally, the third characteristic sound type involves the extremely refined use of clusters, constructed not only in half steps, but also in quarter–tones. The clusters are set in motion through glissandi and through the constant changing of the width of the cluster. These changes in the clusters are reflected in graphic notation involving exact thickness of the beams, thus making them optically perceivable. In the middle section of the composition the material is fragmented and atomized and the various instrumental effects are dynamically manipulated into fluctuating, richly contrasting combinations. This section is written, surprisingly enough, according to principles of post–Webern canonic technique. In the concluding section clusters once again dominate in four–voice, polyphonic layers of sound and noise.

Polymorphia (for 48 string instruments) renounces compositional refinements such as canonic technique or the random selection of attack structures. It is altogether less contrived than *Threnody*, but is more striking in its general impression. Penderecki differentiates his glissando technique even further, using new graphic notation from cardiograms, the so–called fever curves. He also expands his demands on the performers to include such things as playing with heavy bow pressure at the frog so that an ugly grating sound is produced. Near the end of the work it reaches a point of coarse, wild, noisy excess, but the composer neutralizes this with an effect that is extremely simple, but nevertheless highly effective at this point. He follows the tumultous uproar of the full string orchestra with a pure C major chord in radiant *fortissimo.* How ironic!

The String Quartet No. 1, which was written between *Threnody* and *Polymorphia*, introduces the emancipation of noise for the first time into the realm of chamber music. What Penderecki achieved in *Polymorphia* he then carries forward in *Canon* for String Orchestra and Tape, to be sure, in an even more radical graphic notation on graph paper. The performance of the work involves highly complicated use of tape recorders and delayed playbacks. The music played originally is simultaneously recorded and then (with a time delay) played over two loud speakers located behind the audience. The structurally complicated canon runs in retrograde from the middle of the piece to the end. This forward and backward structure is added to the tripartite structure created by the original orchestra performance and the two tape recorded performances. (The score looks more complicated than it actually sounds.)

In 1962 Penderecki finally transfers the results from his three years of experimentation to the large orchestra with the composition of *Fluorescences.* Now a whole army of players is employed: a gigantic string section, woodwinds and brass in groups of four to six, six percussionists each with a powerful collection of drums and a whistle. Electric door bells, musical saws, alarm sirens, and typewriters are included so as to produce the liberated sound, which according to Penderecki lay outside of traditional instrumental design. The Italian Futurists before and after the first world war, who wanted to imbue the world of machines with a musical soul, appear weak in comparison to the ruthless musical demands of Penderecki's *Fluorescences.*

The work is loosly structured in contrasting fields that are juxtaposed in time and space. The formal sections are delineated with acoustic extravagances (saws, bells). In the midst of these extremely cacophonous sections stands an euphonious Intermezzo that could be entitled (recalling Berg's *Wozzeck*) Invention on the Note C. In the course of two and a half minutes this tone is imbued with a broad spectrum of instrumental colors in highly varied temporal and spatial structures. Clusters in quarter–tones and glissandi evoke the final burst of noise. A work without mercy says Penderecki, a final reckoning. He senses that he cannot push this kind of radical ruthlessness any further, not in the technical sense, not in the esthetic sense, and not even in the emotional sense.

Consolidations

For this reason Penderecki undertakes a radical reassessment in this same year, 1962. He composes the *Stabat Mater* for three a cappella choruses. In this composition traditional elements emerge once again, elements which he had not used since 1958, since the *Psalms of David.* He uses the very moment in which he has triumphantly carried his experiments to the very limit, as a time for an act of great boldness in his stylistic development. He consolidates the experiences of his experimental years and the musical fruits of these labors into a stylistic synthesis, which he expands and uses to intensify his own development. His stylistic range extends from quasi–Gregorian chant to clusters, from the major triad to dodecaphony, but he realizes that the new can only have a powerful effect if it appears in the context of the old or familiar.

Writing for three choruses will ultimately become determinative for the *St. Luke Passion*, Penderecki's first major work, in which the *Stabat Mater* occupies a central place. The linearity that is regained in this a cappella chorus belongs to the stylistic spectrum of this first large–scale work just as much as the sounds on the boundary of noise which appear especially in the *Turbae.* Despite some tonal intrusions there is no continuously operative tonality, neither in the sense of major–minor tonality, nor in the sense of the old church modes. Instead there is an ordering based on reference to certain central pitches, as in Bartók. The fact that, already in the first chorus, G, D, and A emerge as principal pitches has less to do with the circle–of–fifths than with the relation of individual parts to the whole of the work. Likewise, in this opening chorus one can clearly recognize the now characteristic duality of color and line. The same duality can be found between clusters in the chorus and small–interval melodic gestures. The row structure of the work is formed from these melodic gestures which, to be sure, bear some resemblance to Gregorian chant, but actually are after–effects of Schönberg.

The basic material of the *Passion* is immediately set forth in the opening chorus *O crux ave*: the germ cell of a descending minor second, the sigh–motive A, A–flat (boys chorus in bars 1 and 2, *crux ave*) and two twelve–tone rows. Row I (two bars later in the bass instruments of the orchestra) consists solely of minor seconds and minor thirds, with the second half being a tritone transposition upwards of the first half. If one treats each note of the row as the beginning of a four–note motive, then each of these motives can be regarded as some form of retrograde–inversion or mirror of another motive. Immediately afterward in measure 7 the boys chorus enters with the second row (*O crux, ave*) which is even more important. This row is first presented as an eight–note series beginning with the sigh–motive (this time E, E–flat). Then the alto voices of the boys chorus and the first chorus add the four notes needed to complete the row — B–flat, A, C, B–natural — or in German note names B–A–C–H, an homage on the part of the young Passion composer to his greatest predecessor. The fact that this row functions somewhat like a cantus–firmus (it is also important in the *Passacaglia, No. 16*) is also reminiscent of the *St. Matthew Passion.* The two rows do not contrast with each other, but rather resemble one other in their structure. The tension of the tritone C–sharp G is moved to the center of Row II. (In this connection the author would refer the reader to his monograph on Penderecki, in which this work is analyzed in great detail.)

The prominence achieved by *The St. Luke Passion* in the middle of the 1960s comes from its compositional expertise and its powerful expressivity. In it Penderecki blends strikingly contrasting materials and also gives us a survey of four musical epochs—the melodic, the linear–polyphonic, the harmonic, and the timbral. In so doing he solves the most intricate stylistic problems and at the same time projects the musical experiments of his early years into his creative future.

Penderecki's creative path leads from the *Passion* directly to the smaller oratorio, *Dies irae*. Hans Werner Henze must have had this work in mind when, in the summer of 1967, he asserted that his Polish colleague had recently written music in which the power of the spiritual and emotional material had testified to a simplicity and essentiality which carried him far beyond the concept of modern music. The most significant parallel work to the *Passion* and the *Dies irae* is Penderecki's first opera, *The Devils of Loudun*. Penderecki profitably uses the experience gained in the composition of the Golgotha music from the *Passion* for dramatic situations such as the exorcism of the devil, the hellish spectacle of the black mass, and the scenes of torture and execution. What is new is the dry bufoonery of the sarcastic musical diction of the surgeon and the pharmacist—obviously based on their predecessors, the captain and the doctor in *Wozzeck*.

At least three especially characteristic works should also be cited for this period of solidification of his individual and unmistakable personal style. The first is the two–part oratorio *Utrenya* (Entombment and Resurrection of Christ). It processes other influences which the composer had drawn from the orthodox Slavic Rites, especially the early masses of Good Friday and Easter Sunday. The quiet meditations of the first part and the radiant, almost uproarious jubilation of the second part are unified through the bonds of language—church Slavic, that corresponds to old Bulgarian. None of Penderecki's previous compositions had sounded more Slavic. Immediately after *Utrenya* Penderecki composes the first of his five symphonies, in which the now forty–year old composer unites all of his orchestra experience into a compendium of his compositional practices. The movements are connected without pause and form a single, large sonata movement: Exposition (*Arché 1*), double development (*Dýnamis 1* and *Dýnamis 2*) and recapitulation (*Arché 2*). It is apparent that he is reaching back to the varied noise spectra of his early period. Repetition of a single tone now assumes structural meaning. He creates the impression of static sound masses by starting with a central tone, fanning out in quarter–tones with seven different rhythms sounded in an overlapping manner and then always returning to the central tone. The first development section is especially rich in contrasts—pointillism next to spreading sound layers. Scurrying chromatic quarter–tones in the strings alone develop into a 46–voice texture. The massing of the voices leads to a furious tumult that is resolved into the repeated tones of *Arché 1*. The second development section employs a scherzo form that is articulated by short chorale–like brass entrances. It also provides space for the raucous unfolding of sounds. The recapitulation serves primarily to allow for a reduction of sound events.

Finally it is necessary to cite the large *Magnificat* of 1974 which directly follows the First Symphony and represents the end of Penderecki's phase of style consolidation. Now he links those elements of his early period that he wanted to preserve with those elements of his compositional technique that were further developed, more differentiated, and almost reminiscent of the techniques of the older masters. This leads once again to a deepening of his musical expressive power in this seven–part work for bass solo, seven male voices, two mixed choruses, boys choir and orchestra. At the very beginning of the work the basic harmonic framework is established. The minor third D–F is the principal interval, soon augmented with the pitches A, and F–sharp, thereby creating a major–minor chord. To this he adds an E–flat and an A–flat in the bass. Thus the D major chord of Bach's *Magnificat* is here veiled with the notes F, E–flat, and A–flat. This chord appears, of course, in many different transpositions. The second movement is a powerful triple fugue, in which Penderecki expands the polyphony to 55 real voices. The first fugue theme, sung by the group of seven male solo voices, is made up of densely layered thirds. These are then sung in glissandi in counterpoint with the first chorus—one group of seven voices in counterpoint with another group of seven voices. The second fugue theme consists of wild chromatic quarter–tones in the chorus and orchestra and is heard more as sound than as theme. The third theme, finally, is a five–voice setting for brass answered in retrograde by the woodwinds. This triple fugue is written with breathtaking skill. Out of its material the Passacaglia of the fifth movement is developed. Over a pedal tone repeated thirteen times, the chorus lines are built up like a pyramid and fanned out in polyrhythms. Using a principle already tested in the first symphony, Penderecki displaces harmony and rhythm symmetrically from a central tone. In the last movement (No. 7) two high trumpets in D evoke the Bach *Magnificat* without actually quoting it. At the end—*In saecula saeculorum*—a twelve tone chord is diatonicized by an E–flat minor chord in the brass insturments. The unison C at the *Amen* is the logical consequence. Nevertheless the *Magnificat* and the short orchestra work *Awakening of Jacob* (1974) provide only the slightest hint of the changes that now lead to radical stylistic metamorphosis.

RETROSPECTIVES

The change of course made ten years earlier from the experiments with musical materials to the *St. Luke Passion* was more or less a matter of expansions, namely the breaking up of sound masses and noise complexes into linear structures. Now Penderecki makes a more radical change that leads him into a completely new stylistic world, into what he himself called his romantic phase. This phase is manifest almost simultaneously in two large works, in the *Violin Concerto No. 1* and in the opera *Paradise Lost*, designated as a *Sacra rappresentazione*. In an uninhibited way they open up the musical idioms of the late nineteenth and early twentieth centuries. Both scores display emotionally expressive music written in a pseudo–tonality that is indebted to post–Wagnerian chromaticism.

With the violin concerto Penderecki seeks and finds a link with the great late romantic concerti from Tchaikovsky and Brahms to Sibelius and Shostakovitch. The work has huge dimensions. Its lyricism pours out in a virtually unending stream, which sometimes reaches dramatic climaxes. The form of the work is a single movement, a broad, freely structured sonata form. (Penderecki will preserve this single–movement form later in other instrumental concerti and in most of his symphonies.) He structures this large form with a revival of Bartók's art of varied development, as it appears in such works as the *Third String Quartet*, which also links all of its sections into a single movement. However, where Bartók crams his constantly imitated material into 17 minutes, Penderecki develops his material in a more sweeping and rhapsodic manner over the course of 40 minutes. Even so, the organic growth from motive to motive, developed out of a single cell, constantly recalls Bartók's technique of metamorphosis.

Twice Penderecki interrupts the chromatically saturated melancholy of this highly expressive music in ponderous 3/2 with intermezzi which have a strange effect. This occurs after the first solo cadenza between the exposition and recapitulation and again in the middle of the second cadenza before the coda. These sections, marked *Tempo di marcia, scherzando,* have a scurrilous, macabre character—like the burlesques in Mahler's *Ninth Symphony* or the tavern music in Berg's *Wozzeck*. Essentially, they remain as enigmatic as the *Allegretto con indifferenza* in Bartók's *Fifth String Quartet*, which may be described as ironic or surrealistic.

Penderecki's style can unfold in an even broader, more expressive manner in the expanded formal relations of the two large acts of the opera *Paradise Lost*, in the dramatic spectacle of the scenes in hell, as well as in the elegiac character of the scenes with Adam and Eve. The choruses carry the main weight of the opera—Satan's minions express themselves in dry, accented *Sprechgesang*; the heavenly hosts express themselves in chaste lyricism or radiant jubilation. An important concept of the puritan idealist John Milton, whose seventeenth–

century work was the inspiration for the opera, was Christ's willingness to be sacrificed to redeem the exiled human couple. Penderecki accompanies Christ's announcement of this with the Bach chorale "Oh great love, oh love without measure' (*O grosse Lieb', o Liebe ohn' alle Masse'*) from the *St. John Passion*, sounded as if it were coming from heaven. The retrospective period in Penderecki's creative life ends in 1980 with the *Te Deum* and the *Second Symphony*, a monumental work in one movement. In the meantime the composer had completely assimilated the late romantic musical idiom. Both works show the effortless incorporation of such things as the fluctuating tonality of Wagner's Nibelungen tetralogy, the advanced chromaticism of Strauss' early works, and also the radiant maestoso glow of Bruckner or the ingenious two–dimensional perspective of Mahler's music. The opening of the Christmas carol "Silent night, holy night" (*Stille nacht, heilige Nacht*), is heard three times penetrating the raging storms and shadows of the *Second Symphony*. The idyllic diatonicism of these passages does not have the effect of a ray of hope, but rather that of a foreign body in the midst of the dark chromaticism of the orchestral events. It is difficult to find any trace of Penderecki's early works in this symphony.

Synthesis

Penderecki must have sensed that deeper penetration into the stylistic world of the late 19th century could dilute and possibly damage his personal style. Therefore in the large *Polish Requiem*, a work that he composed during the next five years, he uses a clear sense of tonality such as that used in the *Te Deum*, but only in the first two movements—in the *Lacrimosa* (1980) and in the *Agnus Dei* (1981). After this, in the *Second Cello Concerto* (1982) and in the main sections of the *Requiem*, which he worked on until 1984, Penderecki reflects again and again on the accomplishments of his own past, on the significant characteristics of his earlier style periods. Therefore he adds many old Penderecki trademarks to the score of his new cello concerto—dry string noises, cluster–clouds in glissandi, scherzando effects in the winds, and aggressive attacks in the percussion instruments—all of this without renouncing the luxuriant sound–ideals of the retrospective compositional years.

In the second cello concerto he extends his examination of the possibilities of single–movement form. The work begins with an *Andante* introduction, followed by the three–fold alternation of *Vivo* and *Lento* sections. The last *Lento* section forms a tender Epilogue. From a larger formal point of view, these three contrasting sectional pairs could be analyzed as an open, freely structured sonata form, even if it is not as clearly delineated as in the *Violin Concerto*. The basic melodic motive consists primarily of minor seconds and tritones in the framework of an essentially non–tonal chromaticism. The *Vivo* sections are mostly thematic and motivic, and are contrapuntally and polyphonically worked out. The slow sections, by contrast, have more of an atmospheric character, indebted more to the romantic spirit. The writing for both the solo instrument and the orchestra has a virtuoso character. Occasionally the writing ventures into regions of artifice, especially during the last *Vivo* section in the seven small, highly sophisticated character studies, which are designated as variations. In these Penderecki combines sound gestures and articulations in a manner recalling some of his attractive earlier works, such as *De natura sonoris* No. 1 (1966) or the *Capriccio for Violin and Orchestra* (1967).

Seen as a whole, the *Second Cello Concerto* and its little brother, the *Concerto for Viola and Orchestra*, written immediately afterward, pave the way for Penderecki's period of synthesis. With full awareness and supreme skill, Penderecki seeks to avoid the danger of becoming an uninhibited traditionalist, a danger that he almost succumbed to in the *Te Deum* and the *Second Symphony*. This could have meant an irreparable loss of identity for the composer. And yet just the opposite occurred. The intensive preoccupation with the music from the end of nineteenth century to the symphonies of Shostakovitch enriched his musical vocabulary. At the same time it led to more differentiation and stylistic independence, and this in turn made it possible for Penderecki to achieve the synthesis which has characterized his music for more than a decade. Now he has command of all the necessary means to express freely and in the most refined detail all the richness of his ideas. This is evident in all realms of his work and is especially apparent in the developmental phase between his third opera, *The Black Mask* (1986), and his fourth opera, *Ubu Rex* (1990/91). The stylistic pluralism, which has been operative since the *Polish Requiem* is enriched in *The Black Mask* by a new dimension, namely the idea of a collage of quotations. Some of these come from the seventeenth century, the century of the Gerhardt Hauptmann play which forms the basis of the libretto. Some come from chorales, songs and dance music. He also cites the medieval *Dies irae* melody as well as the *Dies irae* music from his own *Requiem*, from which he also uses the *Mors stupebit* as counterpoint to the carnival music. This opera is a virtuoso *Danse macabre*, in which the artistically worked out high points of the score are the large ensemble numbers with their hectic confusion. All thirteen characters stammer parts of the text in ad libitum repetitions. The music of this ghostly sonata yields at the end to a real sense of decadence.

The first parts of the *Third Symphony* (*Passacaglia and Rondo*, 1988) and the single–movement *Fourth Symphony* (*Adagio*, 1989) still belong more or less to the style realm of *The Black Mask*, in their dense counterpoint and free tonality (to describe it as atonality would be exaggerated), as well as their complex rhythms and richly differentiated, highly original and unusual instrumentation. In them one senses the last pangs of Penderecki's neo–romantic tonal language. In the English horn solos of the *Fourth Symphony* there are even atmospheric contacts with the sad melody of the third act of *Tristan*.

Since 1990, however, his pluralistic synthesis takes another path in his opera buffa *Ubu Rex*, which he planned for a long time but only now could take in hand. He embarks on what could almost be called a new style phase, to which the *Fifth Symphony* (1991–92) also belongs. Now Penderecki strives for an anti–Romantic posture, inspired by Alfred Jarry's grotesque play *Ubu Roi*, the pilot project of the theater of the absurd. Chromatic excesses are avoided; harmony and melody are sharpened and effortlessly imbedded within clusters and moments of pure tonality, such as the *Polonaise* in B–flat major! Above all Penderecki consistently lightens the dense instrumentation of *The Black Maskers*. The orchestration is characterized by a clear, dry brilliance. Rossini is the model for the large perpetual motion ensembles, for the sense of "brio" which is pushed to the point of absurdity, and certainly for the paradoxical musical dramaturgy. Penderecki plays with Rossini's style without copying it.

One must abandon all thoughts of opera buffa and Rossini when confronted with the *Fifth Symphony* (the "Korean"). Nevertheless, one can regard this work as an orchestral expansion and deepening. Motive construction with sixths and sevenths definitively replaces construction with minor seconds and tritones, which had dominated the earlier style periods. An exception to this is the chromatic, expressive cantilena of the solo horn, which is heard in counterpoint to the three–note, pentatonic Korean song theme on which the cornerstone of the piece, the *Passacaglia*, is built. The virtuoso instrumentation of the work aims at achieving a clear orchestral profile, that shows little similarity to the *Fourth Sympohny*, but does show some similarity to the dry brilliance of *Ubu Rex*. The work builds to a climax with an outburst of the Korean song in majestic radiance, like a chorale of Bruckner. It is played by all seventeen brass instruments (including the four trumpets located in the hall) surrounded by a stormy stream of woodwind and strings and supported by bells and timpani. Significant expansions are represented by the *String Trio* (1991) and the *Quartet for Clarinet and String Trio* (1993), that ends with a profound *Larghetto*, reminiscent of the *Weltschmerz* of late Schubert. This final movement deserves its own stylistic investigation. Penderecki was obviously inspired by the F minor middle section of the *Adagio* from Schubert's *String Quintet in C Major*, to which he adds an F major/F minor sonority veiled with harmonics and neighbor tones. Schubert also writes passages with indefinite harmonies, syncopated rhythms, lines that flow in varied articulations, and a gestural vocabulary of richly contrasting instrumental contours.

The two works premiered in 1995, the *Concerto for Violin No. 2* and the five–movement *Symphony No. 3*, do not chart new stylistic paths. The *Concerto for Violin No. 2* which Penderecki began to compose in 1992, moves in the style realm of the *Fifth Symphony*. In its cyclic structure it joins the ranks of large–dimensioned, one–movement works such as the first violin concerto. However, it does not share the chromatic *Lamento* pathos nor the gloomy drama of the earlier concerto. Instead it is elegaic, more lyric, and more elegant. It is timbrally more differentiated and is more relaxed, reflecting Penderecki's recent experiences, for example with the *Concerto for Flute and Chamber Orchestra* (1992). The creative synthesis of the last decades doubtlessly reaches its peak in the *Third Symphony*. Here in 1995 Penderecki expands the music of the *Symphonic Fragments* (1988), which still stand under the spell of the *Black Mask*, by adding three new movements. In these one can, to be sure, discern the brighter colors and sharper contours of *Ubu Rex* and the *Fifth Symphony*, but now they are seamlessly linked to fragments of music that had been written seven years earlier. This is testimony to the thoughtful and skillful mastery of the composer, who always seems to have his greater success in seamlessly uniting the most diverse elements, even the most extreme characteristics of his own music. The *Rondo* movement of the *Fragments* now becomes the second movement (*Allegro assai*) of the complete Symphony; the *Passacaglia* of the *Fragments* becomes the fourth movement. The new movements are the first, an *Andante* prologue; the third, a melodically rich, spun–out *Adagio*, full of pensive nature music (it may very well be the most significant slow movement that Penderecki has ever composed); and the fifth, a final *Vivace* in which Penderecki achieves orchestral colors that would have made Berlioz envious.

The listener is also struck by the many instrumental solo passages which occur so often in the freely structured orchestral writing that one gets the impression of a concerto for orchestra. Like earlier works, such as the *Second Cello Concerto*, the *Symphonic Fragments*, or the completed Third Symphony, this is music written exclusively for virtuosi. The reason for this is that all three works were commissioned for the jubilees of orchestras—the *Cello Concerto No. 2* for the centennial of the Berlin Philharmonic, the *Fragments* for the fiftieth anniversary of the Swiss Festival Orchestra of Lucerne, and the completed *Third Symphony* for the hundred year celebration of the Munich Philharmonic.

If one were to assign Penderecki's music today to the so–called post–modern movement, then one would have to separate it clearly from the oft–cited new simplicity, playfulness, or especially incomprehensibility. Rather it would be more appropriate to include it in the field of new tonality in the broadest sense, or in a new monumentality as well as a new sound sensibility. Above all it is important to recognize his stylistic independence and to recognize the extraordinary value of his achievement of synthesis in this time at the end of a century of artistic upheaval.

Translated by Allen and Helga Winold

Allen Winold
Bloomington

Penderecki's Violin Concerto No. 2: A Descriptive Analysis

Every new composition creates its own world. It demands to be heard on its own terms, to be understood according to its inner logic, and appreciated for its intrinsic characteristics. Human perception, however, inevitably involves the processes of comparison and categorization. The listener does not mechanically record individual durations, frequencies and timbres, but rather organizes sounds into musical patterns based on experience with previously heard compositions. A descriptive analysis of a new work seeks to reconcile this dichotomy of uniqueness and universality.

Confronted with a work like the *Concerto No. 2 for Violin and Orchestra* of Krzysztof Penderecki, there is a natural tendency to consider the work in comparative terms—to discover similarities and differences between it and other works in the same genre, including the composer's first violin concerto. We shall begin the analysis with some consideration of its relation to other works, but then we shall discuss the unique aspects of the work that contribute to its structure and style.

Historical background and relation to other works

The Concerto was commissioned by the Mitteldeutscher Rundfunk Leipzig (Middle German Radio, Leipzig) and dedicated to the violinist Anne–Sophie Mutter. It was premiered at the opening concert of the fourth MDR Musiksommer on June 24, 1995 in the *Gewandhaus* of Leipzig with Anne–Sophie Mutter as soloist and the MDR Sinfonieorchester under the direction of Mariss Jansons. Two days later the work received its second performance in the *Semper Oper* of Dresden with the same participants. Penderecki began composing the concerto in 1992 and completed it approximately three months before the premiere.

Penderecki's first violin concerto was written roughly twenty years earlier, between 1974 and 1976, and was dedicated to and first performed by Isaac Stern and the Symphony Orchestra of Basel under the direction of Moshe Atzmon. It was commissioned by the *Musikgesellschaft Basel* in celebration of its 100th anniversary.

Aside from obvious similarities in the fact that both concertos were commissioned works and dedicated to and performed by two of the world's renowned violinists, there are other interesting similarities and differences between the two works. For example, there are interesting differences in the playing styles of the two violinists which, consciously or unconsciously, are subtly reflected in the musical gestures of the two works. Both compositions have a balance between lyricism and virtuosity, but the second concerto would seem to have slightly more emphasis on virtuoso passage work and a broader pallette of musical styles.

Both works are in a single connected movement and both are works of significant length—roughly 40 minutes for the first concerto and 35 minutes for the second. The first concerto was the longest instrumental work Penderecki had written until that time.

The first concerto was regarded as representing a significant change in Penderecki's style, especially in its deemphasis of *Klangflächenstil* [sound–mass or sound–surface style], in which timbre effects, some of them involving radically innovative instrumental techniques, become the principal carriers of musical meaning and movement rather than traditional aspects such as rhythm, melody and harmony. In retrospect it can be seen as a logical evolution of Penderecki's stylistic development rather than an abrupt change. The second concerto is even more traditional in its use of musical elements. For example, quarter–tone passages appear in the first concerto but not in the second. A comparison of thematic material from both works reveals that the pitch material in both cases involves ascending and descending chromatic half–step motives separated by a tritone leap (Ex. 1a and 1b). However, rhythm, tempo, articulation and instrumentation make the two passages quite different.

Ex. 1a, Penderecki, *Violin Concerto No. 1*, m. 25

©1976 Schott Musik Internationale. Used by permission.

Ex. 1b, Penderecki, *Violin Concerto No. 2*, m. 37–8

©1995 Schott Musik Internationale. Used by permission.

It is also possible to find similarities between the second concerto of Penderecki and earlier violin concertos. Some of these may be superficial and incidental. For example, the d–minor chord in the cadenza of the second concerto (Ex. 2a) may unavoidably remind listeners of the same chord in the first movement of the Brahms Violin Concerto (Ex. 2b).

Both works have a balance between lyricism and virtuosity, but the second concerto would seem to have slightly more emphasis on virtuoso passage work and a broader pallette of musical styles. Both compositions are notable for idiomatic writing for the violin and colorful use of the orchestra in a way that never covers the soloist.

Ex. 2a, Penderecki, *Violin Concerto No. 2*, cadenza [79]

Ex. 2b, Brahms, *Violin Concerto*, Movement I

FORMAL ASPECTS

Turning to an exploration of the antecedents of single–movement form in earlier literature, we find Beethoven experimenting with attaca connections between the movements of his *String Quartet in C# minor*, Op. 131, or using a cadenza to link the second and third movements of his violin concerto, and Mendelssohn using a sustained B in the bassoon from the ending chord of the first movement of his violin concerto as a link to the introduction of the second movement.

There is strong temptation to try to fit the form of the second concerto of Penderecki into a mold such as an over–all "arch" form similar to that used by Bartók in several works. Instead of trying to match this work to existing historical models, let us first seek to identify the primary form–building elements and present these without reference to existing formal models.

We begin by looking for sections that have well formed musical shape, identifiable character and substantial length, and that recur basically unchanged after intervening contrasting material. This is somewhat difficult in an organically unified work such as the second concerto, in which musical materials constantly recur at least on the motivic level with slight changes in rhythm, pitch and color. However, there is one section which recurs with striking similarity and its importance is furthermore emphasized by its appearance at the very beginning of the work up through section [6]. This music recurs with obvious similarity in sections [30] through [36] and then again in section [86].

Numbers in brackets refers to the composer's own section numbering.

The opening meter (2/2) and tempo *Allegro ma non troppo* (𝅗𝅥=80) are identical in all three sections. The opening thematic material of all three sections is also the same—a four–note repeated figure in half notes (Ex. 3a), then a four–note chromatic half–step scalar figure also in half notes (Ex. 3b). The solemn annunciatory character of the music contributes to its form–holding significance. We designate this section a "motto" section in reference to its functional similarity to at least two famous historical instances of "motto" sections—the repeated chord sections in Mozart's *Magic Flute* overture, and the solemn chordal passages in the first movement of Beethoven's String *Quartet in E–flat Major*, Op. 127. In all three works the "motto" section is used three times to signal significant points in the structure of the work. The difference is that in the Mozart and Beethoven examples they signal sections within a single movement, whereas in the Penderecki concerto they signal large divisions within a single movement.

Ex. 3a, Penderecki, *Violin Concerto No. 2*, m. 1

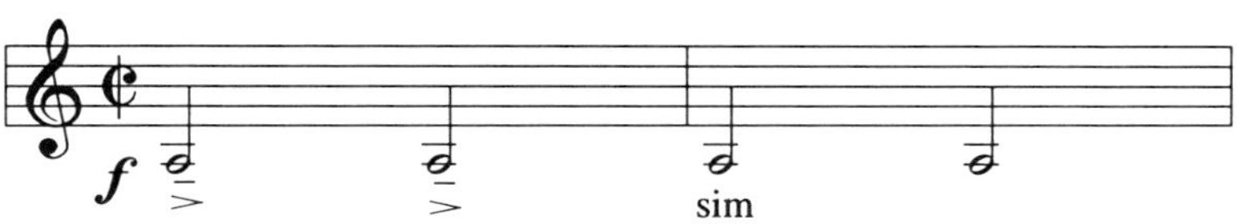

Ex. 3b, Penderecki, *Violin Concerto No. 2*, m. 7

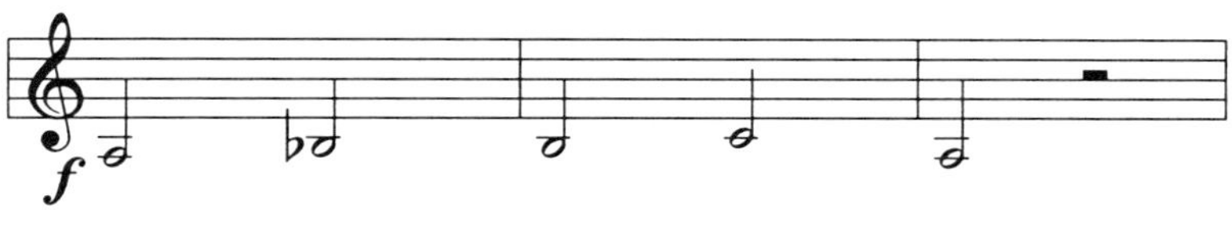

The sections immediately following the first two "motto" sections of the second concerto (sections [7 to 9] and [37]) are also clearly similar. Both feature extended, active passages for the viola section and both begin on the same pitch—B–flat. Both are well formed thematic statements. Two other sections meet our criteria for form–building elements—sections [20 to 22] and [50]. Both feature emphatic statements in the bass instruments, *ff* and *meno mosso*.

In this initial survey we can also identify the location of the lengthy solo violin cadenza at section [79] near the end of the work and then we have the following preliminary outline for the second concerto:

Table I
Preliminary Outline of Concerto No. 2

Sections	Description
[0 to 6]	Motto section
[7 to 9]	Thematic section
[10 to 19]	———
[20 to 22]	Peroration or concluding section
[23 to 29]	———
[30 to 36]	Motto section II
[37]	Thematic section
[38 to 49]	———
[50]	Peroration or concluding section
[51 to 78]	———
[79]	Cadenza
[80 to 85]	———
[86]	Motto section III
[87 to 93]	

Let us describe in greater detail the sections we have established and speculate on the sections that lie in between. Motto section I presents the two basic thematic cells described above and develops these in the string section through inversion, beginning a tritone above on E–flat, and imitation. This leads to the pp entrance of the solo violin in section 2 and a long sustained low A, out of which grows a tranquillo theme (Ex. 4a) based on chromatic half–step motion derived from the material in the Motto section and leaps of a major sixth or a minor third. This material is developed and leads with crescendo to a *ff* climax at section [5], where the pitch A is vigorously enunciated with dotted rhythms and octave leaps. The close of Motto section I brings a return of the chromatic theme (Ex. 3b) and a long diminuendo.

Ex. 4, Penderecki, *Violin Concerto No. 2*, m. 2–6

The viola thematic passage, m. 7 to 9 (Ex. 5) marked *Allegro vivace* (𝅗𝅥 = 80), is punctuated by answering figures in the low clarinet and bass clarinet and later by staccato chords in the brass and tone clusters in the strings and winds.

Ex. 5, Penderecki, *Violin Concerto No. 2*, m. 7–1

The solo violin enters with neighbor figures on pitches C and C–flat (Ex. 6) that are similar in character to the viola passage. The material is elaborated and developed in various ways including two short virtuoso candenzas for the solo violin and references to the chromatic scalar figures of the opening. An orchestral passage featuring dotted rhythms at rehearsal number 13 brings this musical unit to a close.

Ex. 6, Penderecki, *Violin Concerto No. 2*, m. 10–1

The solo violin enters with a new tempo (*Allegro vivace*), and a theme (Ex. 7), that sounds fresh even though it begins with a neighbor passage on the same pitches C and D–flat used in Ex. 6. This material is elaborated and developed with references to the basic chromatic scalar figures, chordal punctuation and vigorous dotted–note figures. This musical unit ends with a crescendo that leads to the orchestral conclusion or peroration.

Ex. 7, Penderecki, *Violin Concerto No. 2*, m. 14–1

This conclusion is marked *meno mosso*, (♩= 64) and features leap figures (Ex. 8) in the low instruments, *fortissimo*. At rehearsal number 21 the scalar figures return and are developed along with other material in increasingly fast tempo leading to a *meno mosso* section at rehearsal number 23 with a soaring high solo violin passage over quiet syncopated chords in the strings. This musical unit ends with a magical sounding sonority ppp with clusters in high strings and celesta with other delicate percussion instruments, and a high D in the solo violin.

Ex. 8, Penderecki, *Violin Concerto No. 2*, m. 20–1

Sections 24 to 29 are played by constantly changing chamber music combinations of solo violin and varied instrumental groupings—for example four–part settings with solo violin, clarinet, horn and low strings at rehearsal number 27. At some points the solo violin plays alone in rubato passages. The musical material consists of references to previously heard figures, virtuoso passages for the solo violin based on both old and new musical figures, and anticipations of material which will be thematically treated in later sections, for example, the rhythmic figures in the flute in m. 27–4 which will be heard in the solo violin at rehearsal number 38.

How shall we designate the musical units described above? It would certainly be possible to make a case for something at least approaching the model of sonata form in the second concerto. In the following analysis we use terms associated with sonata form analysis, but in so doing do not necessarily imply that Penerecki had a "pre–conceived sonata form mold" into which he simply poured material. With these conditions in mind we suggest the following outline given in Table II for the material discussed to this point [vs=violin solo, o=orchestra].

Motto section II is again devoted to repeated figures and scalar figures, but it has a gentler, more lyrical character than Motto section I. In section [37] the viola section plays the main theme, this time punctuated by repeated notes in the timpani. The theme is written in sixteenth notes in 4/4, with a tempo marking of ♩ = 92, but the sounding durations are identical to the eighth notes in 2/2 with tempo marking of 𝅗𝅥 = 92 in section [7].

Table II

Outline of the first 29 sections of the Concerto No. 2

Sections	**Inst**	**Tempo and/or character**	**Descriptions**
[beginning to 2]	O	Allegro ma non troppo 2/2 (𝅗𝅥 = 80)	Motto section I
[3 to 4]	VS/O	Tranquillo	First solo entrance
[5 to 6]	O		Climax and diminuendo
[7 to 9]	O	Allegro vivace 2/2 (𝅗𝅥 = 92)	Main theme group
[10 to 12]	VS/O		Second theme group
[13]	O		Concluding passage
[14 to 19]	VS/O	Allegro vivace 2/2 (𝅗𝅥 = 120)	Closing theme group
[20 to 23]	O	Changing	Codetta or Peroration
[24 to 29]	VS/O	Changing	Development section

If the preceding material has suggested the exposition and development of a sonata form we may expect that we have arrived at the recapitulation section. However, full–blown recapitulation sections are not to be expected to the same degree in 20th century works as they were in earlier periods. Elliott Carter and others have suggested that the ubiquitous presence of recordings in our musical life, and the possibility they afford of limitless repetition has eliminated the necessity for building literal or near literal repetition into the structure of a modern work. In any case, what Penderecki gives us here from section [38] up to the cadenza of section [79] is a series of what might be called "character pieces" in contrast to the "theme groups" of sections [7] through [29]. We outlined these in Table II and discuss them in greater detail in the following paragraph. The viola main theme is abbreviated considerably and leads to a dance–like passage in which the solo violin plays a theme based on the same dactylic rhythm (eighth – sixteenth–sixteenth) heard in sections [27] through [29] (Ex. 9), accompanied by viola, bass, clarinet, and bass clarinet. The dance continues in an *Allegro vivo* passage for solo violin alone [39] and then in a passage for solo violin, flute, and tam–tam.

Ex. 9 Penderecki, *Violin Concerto No. 2* (m.[38–1])

A jaunty dotted–note theme marked *scherzando* is heard in the high woodwinds in section [41] and this playful mood continues in an extended passage through section [49]. The passage is characterized by lively idiomatic passage work for the solo violin and colorful, constantly changing orchestration. The forward motion is impelled through increasingly fast note values, and faster tempos as well as by sections of changing meter (3/8, 2/4, 5/8 in bars 47–3 to 47–5).

In section [50] we hear ponderous major sixth leaps, *ff* and *molto meno mosso* (♩=70) in the low instruments that are similar to those in section [20] (Ex.8), but whereas the original passage served as a peroration or conclusion, here the passage is heard as an interruption, especially because it is approached without *crescendo*. The passage is almost Shakespearean in its dramatic character, as though it were music accompanying the sudden solemn appearance of a Prospero or an Oberon in the midst of the playful antics of other–worldly creatures. Dramatic contrasts such as this should not surprise us, coming from the pen of one of the century's most gifted musico–dramatic composers.

A diminuendo at the end of this section leads without pause to an *espressivo* passage for the celli (Ex. 10). Once again Penderecki shows his great skill in using the same melodic figures (chromatic half–steps, leaps of a major sixth) to evoke a totally different emotion. The solo violin enters with high neighbor figures in triplet sixteenths, accompanied by a colorful orchestral tapestry of swooping harmonic *glissandi* in the strings, and punctuated by high parallel thirds in woodwinds, celesta, and bells. The song–like passage from section [51] through [57] could be extracted as a separate slow movement were it not for the fact that it does not come to a conclusion, but instead leads without pause to a transition in sections [58] through [63].

Ex. 10 Penderecki, *Violin Concerto No. 2* (m [51–1])

This transition section is based on rapid three–note chromatic scalar figures, tone clusters and virtuoso passage work with double stops and extensive leaps in the solo violin. The end of the transition, section [63] marked *scherzando*, features harmonics and trills in the solo violin. A *bariolage* (rapid string crossing) passage leads to a set of three colorful character pieces presented in succession.

The first of these is marked *poco meno mosso* and *capriccioso* and has an insouciant, *burleske* character created through the use of staccato leaps, trills, and extended grace note passages in the solo violin *con sordino*. The light staccato accompanying passages in woodwinds and low strings include a figure heard in bass clarinet and then in bassoon that sounds almost like mocking laughter. Closer examination of this figure (four fast repeated notes, an ascending minor third, and a return to the original pitch) shows that it is the same as the opening figure of the bassoon solo in the following section.

The second character piece [67] (Ex. 11) sounds like a rustic folk dance. This is accomplished partly by the use of solo bassoon, an instrument that is frequently called upon for characteristic rustic passages as in Beethoven's *Pastorale Symphony*. It also comes from the fact that for the first time in the concerto we have an extended passage that sounds almost as if it were tonal, D minor in this case. The bassoon solo is accompanied by sparse chords in brass and strings, and chromatic scalar figures in high woodwinds and later in low strings pizzicato.

Table III
Outline of sections 30 to 93 of the Concerto No. 2

Section	Inst	Tempo and/or character	Description
[30 to 36]	VS/O	*Tempo primo* 2/2 (𝅗𝅥 = 80)	Motto section II
[37]	O	(♩ = 92) Main theme group	
[38 to 40]	VS/O	*Allegretto poco sostenuto* 3/4	"Dance–like"
[41 to 49]	VS/0	*piu animato, scherzando* some metric changes	"Scherzo"
[50]	VS/O	*molto meno mosso* 4/4 (♩ = 70)	"Interruption"
[51 to 57]	VS/O	*Andante espressivo* 4/8 (♪= 48)	"Song–like" ("slow movement")
[58 to 62]	VS/O	*Vivace* 4/8	Transitional
[63]	VS/O	*Scherzando* 3/8	Transitional
[64 to 66]	VS/O	*poco meno mosso,* some other changes tempo and meter *capriccioso*	Quasi–thematic and transitional
[67]	O	*Vivace* 3/4	"Folk Dance I"
[68 to 72]	VS/O	*Scherzando* 2/2 (𝅗𝅥 = 120)	"Folk Dance II" ("Mock fugue)
[73 to 74]	VS/O	*feroce*	Transitional
[75 to 76]	VS/O	*Vivacissimo*	Transitional
[77 to 79–1]	O O	VS/O 3/2	Chordal affirmation, Solo passage Chordal affirmation
[79–2]	VS	free	Cadenza
[80]	VS/O O	3/4 (*Allegro*) *Andante con moto*	Chordal affirmation and diminuendo
[81 to 85]	VS/O	*Sostenuto* 3/4 later 4/4	"Elegy"
[86]	VS/O	*Tempo primo*	Motto section III
[87 to 89]	VS/O	*dolce*	"Lyric passage"
[90]	VS/O	*piu animato scherzando* 3/4	"Scherzo reminiscence"
[91 to 92]	VS/O	*quasi di lontano*	"Elegy reminiscence"
[93]	VS/O		Coda

Ex. 11 Penderecki, *Violin Concerto No. 2* (m. [67–1])

The final character piece in this grouping of three pieces is even more resolutely tonal. It begins in section [68] with a simple melody in B minor (or B phrygian) in the solo violin (Ex. 12). In section [69] the same melody is played in G major by the viola section in a fairly literal inversion. It is accompanied by counterpoint in the solo violin. First violins sound the melody in its original form in section [70] accompanied by counterpoint in the solo violin and the viola section. Finally in section [71] the theme is heard in D minor, sounded in canon by low strings and high woodwinds with other contrapuntal accompanying lines.

Ex. 12. Penderecki, *Violin Concerto No. 2* (m.[68–1])

In the course of hearing this passage the listener undoubtedly will be struck by the thought that this might be fugal. Further listening will probably bring the realization that it is not based on the seamless texture of a fugue by Bach, but rather has more similarities to the fugue in Mozart's *Musikalischer Spaß*, with its rustic "four–square" theme and its overly obvious fugal entrances. Penderecki has shown us in many memorable passages of both instrumental and vocal works that he is a master of counterpoint. In this passage he seems more concerned with establishing a jovial mood than he is in creating a display of learned counterpoint.

In the transition beginning in section [73] we return to the chromatic world of the rest of the piece with rapid chromatic scalar passages, tone clusters, and vigorous triplet passages in the solo violin. Beginning in section [75] there is an increase in tempo, dynamics and tension culminating in section [77] with a powerful chordal affirmation repeated several times in the full orchestra. A solo passage in section [78] lightens the texture momentarily, until in section

[79] another chordal affirmation in full orchestra leads to the extended solo violin cadenza.

In the grand tradition of violin concerto cadenzas, this cadenza artfully recalls and recasts the principal thematic material of the concerto. At the same time it provides the soloist with a marvelous vehicle for the display of all of the traditional virtuoso techniques—rapid passage work, wide leaps, trill passages, and double, triple, and quadruple stops, and even some non–traditional techniques such as *ponticello*, the "glassy" effect, produced by bowing near the bridge.

In section [80] we hear the final chordal affirmations answered by quad–ruple stops in the solo violin and then later underlined by rapidly repeated notes in the timpani. A cluster chord with an underlying timpani roll is sustained with a long diminuendo leading in section [81] to a simple but enormously expressive melody in the solo violin (Ex. 13). We have labelled this section "Elegy," not because of any specific statement from the composer, but rather because of its character and because it inevitably reminds us of one of the great concerto works of the first part of the 20th century, the Berg *Violin Concerto* dedicated "to the memory of an angel," referring to the death of the daughter of his friend, Alma Mahler.

The melody begins in D minor, but even in the opening measure we are reminded of the chromatic world through the E–flat–D–E–flat neighbor figure in second violins. Later the steadily moving quarter notes of the solo violin part also recall the non–diatonic world. In section [82] there is a passage in which the solo violin plays both a sustained melody on an upper string and an accompanying faster moving counterpoint on a lower string. In sections [83 to 89] the melody returns in the high woodwinds accompanied by counterpoint in the solo violin. It is extended with other material such as the *espressivo*

Ex. 13. Penderecki, *Violin Concerto No. 2,* section [81]

duo between solo violin and solo oboe in the middle of section [86] or the soaring solo violin melody over the gently syncopated C–sharp minor chords (with G in the bass) in section [87]. Section [90] brings a gentle reminiscence of the *scherzando* mood of earlier sections and section [91] brings the final sounding of the elegiac D minor melody. The work quietly moves to its close with a return of the chromatic scalar figure from the Motto sections and two soundings of the E–flat to D neighbor figure in a solo viola. It ends with a *pp* chord consisting of the pitch D in several octaves colored only by one other note, the A in the first oboe.

Summarizing our view of the form of the work we can say that the three Motto sections serve to divide it into four connected parts, an introduction, a "sonata–like" section devoted to the exploration of musical materials, a "suite–like" part devoted to the presentation of charateristic pieces, and an Epilogue. An even broader view of the work could be taken, emphasizing its over–all arch form.

Regarding the tonal form of the work, we note first that the work ends with a clear emphasis on D, and that D is also emphasized in sections [35] and [67]. Next we note that the emphasized pitch at the opening of the first and last Motto sections is A, suggesting possibly a dominant function for this pitch. Even in the second motto section where the pitch B is emphasized, the bass instruments sound a low pedal A.

The experienced listener hearing this work for the first time should be aware of the special placement of the large cadenza. In classical and romantic concertos the cadenza usually appears near the end of a movemment, and indeed serves to signal approaching closure. In this concerto the music following the cadenza is substantial in length and content. The over–all balance of the work demands a lengthy release of the tension created by the work as a whole and the cadenza in particular.

Stylistic Aspects

In the course of our descripion of formal aspects we touched briefly on some stylistic aspects. In this section we shall delve more deeply into some of the elements of Penderecki's musical language in this concerto.

Orchestration, Dynamics, and Texture. The *Concerto for Violin and Orchestra No. 2* is scored for strings; woodwinds in pairs with the second player of each instrumental section doubling on piccolo, cor anglais, bass clarinet, and double bassoon respectively; a brass section of four horns, two trumpets, and three trombones; timpani; and a percussion section of triangle tree, suspended cymbals, tamtam, tomtoms, bass drum with cymbal, tubular bells, glockenspiel, xylophone, and marimbaphone. As with other works of Penderecki, including the first violin concerto, the full orchestral *tutti* is heard in only relatively rare examples such as the chordal affirmations of sections [77] through [80]. Instead Penderecki uses constantly changing combinations of instruments.

In contrast to Penderecki's early instrumental works which explored instrumental effects in an extreme manner, the instrumental writing used in the second concerto is generally traditional. One of the most interesting instrumental effects used in the work is illustrated in bars [9–1] to [9–5] and elsewhere in the Concerto. A short, three–note figure is repeated 5 times by the celli, one stand at a time in rapid succession, first running from the first stand to the fifth stand and then in reverse. This creates both an interesting effect that is both aural and visual or spatial. Other interesting instrumental aspects include the harmonic glissandi of section [51], the use of ponticello in the cadenza, and, throughout the work, the imaginative writing for the percussion section. Some percussion instruments such as the tam–tam are also used to signal important formal divisions of the work.

One of the most important reasons for the success of this concerto and other instrumental works of Penderecki is his thorough understanding of the idiomatic possibilities of instruments, especially the violin, his own instrument. Though he writes works which may challenge even the greatest of performers, he writes *for* the instrument, not *against* it.

Dynamics in this work are well worked out and contribute to the formal clarity of the work as well as its emotional expressivity.

Turning to the texture of this work, we find that there are a limited number of places where Penderecki writes in such traditional textures as block chords [77], melody and chordal accompaniment [23], or linear counterpoint [68] to [72]. A significant number of passages of this concerto are written in kaleidoscopic or constantly varying motivic counterpoint. Let us briefly analyze section [10] as an example of this. The solo violin enters with an eighth note neighbor figure over a cluster chord in the horns and trumpets and a rapid passage of sixteenth notes in the flute. As the first violin rests for a bar the bass clarinet sounds short, three–note chromatic scalar passages in triplet eighth notes. The solo violin re–enters and expands and elaborates on the neighbor figure accompanied first by the viola section with motives from section [7];then by an "accretion" chord (in this instance consisting of alernating fifths and minor seconds) in the violins. The term "accretion" chord indicates that instruments enter one at a time with the notes of a chord and sustain these while other instruments add their notes to the chord. At the very end of the section high woodwinds sound a 10–note chromatic scale in double–tongued triplet eighth notes. The texture here displays a constant element, the solo violin passage, with varying textural elements cast against it. In other passages all of the textural elements may be in flux.

Rhythm and Melody: Significant portions of the second large part of work are in *alla breve* meter and *allegro* tempo. In the third major part, there is more variety in meter and tempo to fit the individual character pieces. The

Introduction and Epilogue are in a slow tempo.

In the description of formal aspects we briefly mentioned aspects of Penderecki's melodic technique. Let us now examine a typical passage to study this in greater detail. The main theme in the violas in section [7] (Ex. 5) illustrates several techniques typical for this concerto. It begins by presenting a short motive followed by a rest and then a slightly longer version of the motive. After another rest the motive is continued and elaborated into a longer passage. This melodic process sounds completely natural and indeed almost like speech in its structure.

Turning to smaller aspects we find that this passage, like many in the concerto, is drawn from a relatively limited set of melodic seed motives; chromatic scalar figures, neighbor figures, leaps of a tritone, and octave displacements account for most of the pitch material. Rhythmically we can observe Penderecki's use of the technique of repetition with metric displacement. For example, in measure 7–6 we find a six–note figure running from G–flat to C beginning on the strong first quarter of the measure. This six–note figure is then literally repeated, but now it begins on the weak fourth quarter of the measure. This technique is by no means new with Penderecki, rather it can be traced back to Bartók, Brahms, or even to Baroque and Renaissance composers. Penderecki uses it however, in an especially natural and convincing manner in many places in the work.

Harmony: We have already indicated the relatively infrequent use of chordal textures in the Concerto, but it is still appropriate to examine, at least briefly, Penderecki's harmonic style in this work. We can identify four principal types of harmonic writing. The first type is one that is present in many of Penderecki's works—the cluster chord built of seconds. Examples appear in the Motto sections (Ex. 14a) and throughout the work. An interesting type of harmonic writing used with a fair amount of frequency can be analyzed as a diminished seventh chord with an added note (Ex. 14b). This description is not meant, however, to imply that Penderecki necessarily created these chords in this manner, only that they may be analyzed in this way. Several melodic passages such as [78–1] may also be related to the diminished seventh chord with an added note. Even more traditional are the occasional but striking use of major and minor triads such as the lyric passage in Ex. 14c or the climactic chordal affirmations of Ex. 14d. At the other extreme are highly dissonant chords based on minor seconds separated by fifths or tritones as in Ex. 14e.

Ex. 14a Penderecki, *Violin Concerto No. 2* (m.7)

Ex. 14b Penderecki, *Violin Concerto No. 2* (m.[8–5])

Ex. 14c Penderecki, *Violin Concerto No. 2* (m.[33–1])

Ex. 14d Penderecki, *Violin Concerto No. 2* (m.[77–1])

Ex. 14e Penderecki, *Violin Concerto No. 2* (m. [77–5])

Summary and Evaluation

The *Concerto No.2 for Violin and Orchestra* of Krzysztof Penderecki is a magnificent contribution to the violin concerto literature of the twentieth cenury. Its consumate melding of tradition and innovation makes it accessible to the inexperienced listener and fascinating for the more experienced connossieur. It presents great challenges for soloist and orchestra, but these are realistic and worthwhile. Coming at the end of a century that has not seen as many signficant works for violin and orchestra as the nineteenth century, it could very well represent for the second half of the century what the Berg Concerto did for the first half of the century.

Ray Robinson
West Palm Beach

String Trio and Sinfonietta

Begun at the time Penderecki was working on his fourth opera *Ubu Rex*, and completed shortly after the opera's premiere in Munich, the *String Trio* (1990–91) marked a new style in the composer's chamber works. Prior to the Trio, the last major work in this medium was the *String Quartet No. 2*, completed in 1968 during the period of the opera *The Devils of Loudun* and the oratorio *Utrenya*.[1] The Trio is a work from this later style period.

Commissioned by the Cultural Ministry of Baden–Württemberg, the Trio was composed in 1990–91 and premiered on November 15, 1991 by the *Deutsches Streichtrio* [German String Trio] at the International Festival of Contemporary Music in the French city of Metz. An earlier reading of the second movement, the first to be completed, was presented by the German String Trio on September 24, 1991, at the 34th Warsaw Autumn Festival. Soon after the premiere Penderecki revised the work for string orchestra and named it *Sinfonietta per archi*, an idea that had occurred to him earlier when the Trio was in its formative stage. "When I was writing the *String Trio* I wanted to do an orchestral version anyway," he admitted in 1995 during an interview in Ann Arbor, Michigan.[2] Penderecki conducted the first performance of this new version in Warsaw on February 16, 1992, with the Sinfonia Varsovia. It has since become one of his most frequently performed works.

FORMAL CHARACTERISTICS

The obvious external form of the Trio is sectional (see Charts I and II) but the method of construction that brings unity to the work is much more subtle. There are elements in both movements that could suggest some kind of expanded sonata–allegro scheme. It might also be appropriate to identify an "arch"[3] construction in movement one since the scheme A–B–C–B–A could lead to this conclusion. With the rather clear return of the fugue–like theme in the final section of second movement, it is tempting to speculate that the composer might have had a sonata form in mind. However, rather than try to match what the composer has done formally in this work with historical models, in our analysis we will discuss the construction of the work from the evidence the composer leaves us in the score and let the readers draw their own conclusions.

The organization of the first movement (see Chart I) is determined as much

Chart I

Formal Elements in Movement 1

A (m. 1–13 Introductory	**B (m. 14–46 [*Vivo*]**	**C (m. 47–64) [*Adagio*]**	**D (m. 65–105) [*Vivo*]**	**E (m. 106–113) [*Adagio*]**
1.1 Subsection 1 11 note chords (m. 1–3) Viola cadenza (m.4) (Tonal center of G)	2.1 Subsection 1 3 note cell from viola cadenza is prominent	3.1 Subsection 1 cell motive is promi–nent	4.1 Subsection 1 Linear cells punctu–ated with pizzacato motive	5.1 Subsection 1 Recap of intro in miniature
1.2 Subsection 2 14 note chords (m.5–8) Cello cadenza (m. 9) Minor 3rd prominent	2.2 Subsection 2 2 note cell octave dis–placement is intro–duced	3.2 Subsection 2 Cell motive in widely disjunct placement	4.2 Subsection 2 Cell motive alternates with block chords	5.2 Subsection 2 Cell motive inverted, movement ends with one measure melodic and rhythmic motive of fugue theme in Movement 2
1.3 Subsection 3 10 note chords (m. 10–12) Violin cadenza (m. 13) Minor 2nd prominent				

by changes in tempo and timbre as it is by musical content. There are also elements here that take the listener back to the Baroque *concerto grosso* form, especially in the "block chord" figure that prevails throughout the movement and gives the listener the feeling of a ritornello. If one considers the opening (m. 1–13) as an introductory section [with the block chord and linear cadenza passages alternating with one another, there is a tendency to do so], the movement breaks down formally into five sections: Introduction (A), Vivo (B), Adagio (C), Vivo (B1) and Adagio (A1). Sections two and four and three and five are related on the basis of tempo, motivic material and the tonality of G. The way the final section (m. 106–131) is constructed gives the listener the feeling of a truncated reprise or recapitulation. There is one other characteristic of the movement that deserves consideration: the musical ideas that form the basis for the movement are clearly introduced in the opening section.

The thematic elements of the opening movement also dominate the form and content of movement two which, in contrast to the first movement, has only one designated tempo change: *poco meno mosso* at m. 198. Like the opening movement, the tonal center of G is prominent throughout and the motivic material upon which it is based has already been introduced in the opening section (A) of movement one. Formally, the second movement falls into five divisions (A, B, C, D, A), with the final section representing a clear attempt at recapitulation. The Trio takes approximately 12 minutes to perform. As there is no pause between movements one and two, the many changes in tempo give the work the feeling of one continuous movement.

THE MUSICAL CONTENT

The manner in which Penderecki crafts the musical content in the opening section of movement one is especially interesting. Consisting of three subsections in which fiercely executed string chords at the tempo marking *Allegro molto* are followed by cadenzas in each of the instruments in the order viola, violoncello and violin, the work catches the immediate attention of the listener. The block chords consume nine notes of the chromatic scale (all except a, c and f) and are played as quadruple stops (Ex. 1). [The parallel passage in *Sinfonietta* consists of ten notes.] These validictory chords are followed by a slower and more expressive cadenza–like passage (*Andante*) in the viola. It is the motivic material from this sub–section that forms the basis for one of the key musical ideas of the Trio; the seminal motive of two–, three– and four–note cells of consecutive minor seconds (See Ex. 2). It is this motive that will form the basis for sections 2 and 4 of the first movement and the fugue–like theme that opens movement two. As he has done consistently when construct

Ex. 1, Penderecki, *String Trio*, Viola cadenza, m. 4

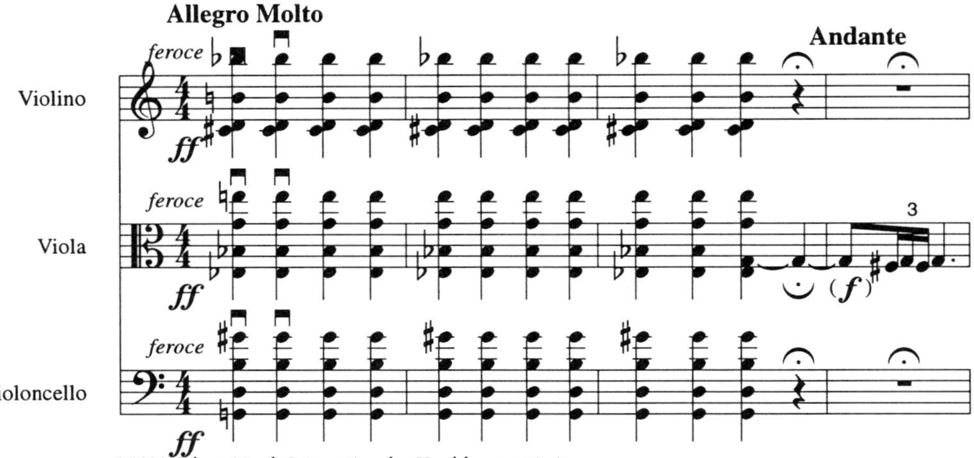

©1991 Schott Musik Internationale. Used by permission.

ing his "linear events" Penderecki creates an atonal texture which sounds both melodic and expressive (e.g. through the use of narrow intervals, octave displacement at the interval of the minor second and the legato character of the writing).

Ex. 2, Penderecki, String Trio, Viola cadenza, m. 4

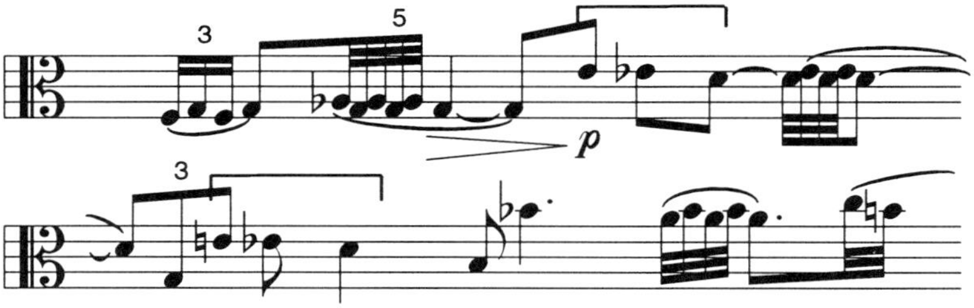

The process is repeated again in the second subsection (m. 5–9) with some changes. This time there are fourteen instead of eleven introductory chords and the cadenza is given to the violoncello. The tempo marking is *Allegretto* and the overall style of the cadenza changes from rhapsodic to capricious and playful. Here the interval of the minor third, which will become the seminal interval for the fugue–like theme of movement two, is introduced. There are also other musical ideas heard here which will contribute significantly to the unity of the work: the triplet figures and, of course, the "cell" motive. In contrast to the opening cadenza in the viola, where the style is very expressive, here the 'cello is instructed to execute idiomatic string techniques like *spiccato* and *sul ponticello* and to play the passage *poco rubato e capriccioso* (Ex. 3).[4]

Ex. 3, Penderecki, *String Trio*, Violoncello cadenza, m. 9

In the third sub–section, Penderecki writes 10 block chords and gives the cadenza to the violin. Again the idiomatic quality of the instrument is explored to its fullest with double, triple and quadruple stops (Ex. 4). This allows a demonstration of the violin's unique idiomatic characteristics and its inherent possibilities. The linear writing is also dominated by the two–and three–note cells that were first heard in the viola cadenza and the interval of the augmented fourth (tritone) that will also form part of the fugue–like theme of the final movement. This opening section ends as it began, with a four–note block chord passage, this time in the violin.

Ex. 4, Penderecki, *String Trio*, Violin cadenza, m. 13

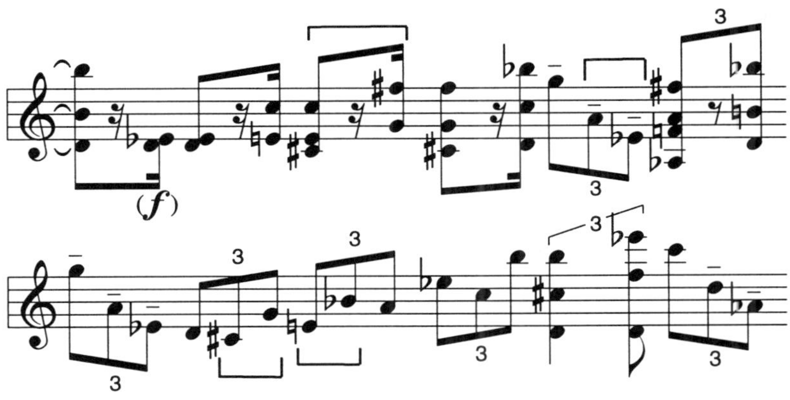

Two characteristics of this introductory section (A) are of special interest and deserve further comment. One is the unique and individual character which the composer creates in these solo cadenza passages: expressive and rhapsodic in the viola, playful and capricious in the violoncello, and rhythmic and virtuostic in the violin, each in keeping with the idiomatic qualities of the instrument. As these ideas are developed throughout the Trio they will provide the unity and variety which are a special characteristic of Penderecki's art. The second is the composer's tendency to use the opening section of his works as an opportunity to introduce musical materials upon which the entire work will be based. This is not a new feature in Penderecki's compositional style. One observes it in many works, but perhaps the best–known example is the *St. Luke Passion* where the "sigh" motive in the opening measure of the boy's chorus (the falling minor second), the two tone rows (Cantus firmus I and II) which establish the linear basis of the work, and the B–A–C–H motive, heard more than 100 times throughout the Passion, are all introduced in the work's opening section.[5] This practice is followed in the String Trio as well: The block chords in the opening measures, the two, three and four note "cells" in the viola cadenza, the interval of the minor third in the violoncello cadenza, the tri–tone in the violin cadenza, and the idiomatic character of the string writing, all key elements in the overall construction of the work, are introduced in this opening section.

The next section (B) (Vivo, 4/8, ♪=150) brings a capricious quality to the piece. The three–note "cells" introduced by the viola in measure four provide the primary linear material. Again the instruments are treated idiomatically, first by having them play *con sordino*, then *sul ponticello* and finally *pizzacato.* Further variety is introduced by the articulation (legato, staccato) and motivic inversion created by the composer. Gradually the tonal material is expanded from chromatic to more widely disjunct linear writing as the three–note cell motive is developed. After a one measure transition (*poco rallentando*), a new section (C) begins (Adagio, ♪=72). This might be considered as the first of two trio–like slow sections which are based on material introduced in the viola cadenza. The narrow linear intervals of the three–note cells are expanded as the motive is developed. A second subsection (4/8, ♪=54) of short duration (eight measures) offers wide intervallic expression of the basic material in a syncopated rhythmic texture and ends on a widely spaced fermata chord exploiting the upper tessitura of each instrument.

A second fast section (B1) (Vivo, 3/8, ♪=130) based on the primary cell motive follows. In contrast to the earlier Vivo section, a much wider dynamic range is exhibited this time. Two–and three–note *pizzacato* motives initially punctuate the linear texture and lead to references to the block chord texture of the opening measure. Again the idiomatic colors unique to stringed instruments provide aural variety through *pizzacato*, *tremolo*, *arco battuto* and *tallone.*[6] The section ends fff with the block chord motive appearing in triplet figures. The cantilene from the viola cadenza introduces the second slow trio–like section (A1) (*Adagio*, 4/8, ♪=72) but here there is also a reference to the block chords of the opening in the second measure. The three–note cells provide the pimary linear material for this section which ends pianissimo as the viola introduces in a one measure coda the melodic and rhythmic motive that will serve as the model for the fugue–like theme of movement two which follows attacca (Ex. 5).

Ex. 5, Penderecki, *String Trio*, basic motive for fugue–like theme, m. 131

Movement Two opens with a 28–measure fugue–like theme (A) in the viola that is derived from three motives from the opening section of the work: the minor third, the tri–tone, and the three–note cell motive. (Ex. 6) The key compositional device here is motivic development. The violin follows the viola "exposition" with a 24–bar statement of the theme beginning not on "G", which

Ex. 6, Penderecki, *String Trio*, Movement 2

characterized the viola passage, but on "D" which gives the suggestion of an exposition section some credibility. But just when the cello is expected to enter with the fugue theme, Penderecki surprises the listener and crafts a development–like section that is built on prominent elements from the first movement: 2–, 3– and 4–note cell motives, block chords and fragments of the fugue–like theme. With the pizzacato entrance of the cello at bar 53, the linear character of the fugue is confronted by a vertical texture that is taken unmistakenly from the block chords of the opening section of the work. The style and texture of this new section are created through their juxtaposition and capricious interplay. A variation on the fugue theme is then picked up by the violoncello

Chart II

Formal Elements in Movement II

A (m. 1–96 [*Vivace*]	**B (m. 96–159** [*Vivace*]	**C (m. 159–197)** [*Poco piu mosso*]	**D (m. 198–232)** [*Poco meno mosso*]	**E (m. 233–307)** [*Vivace*]
1.1 Subsection 1 Fugue–like statement in viola (m. 1–28) Tonal Center of G	2.1 Subsection 1 Cello develops motives from mov't. 1 (m. 96–128)	3.1 Subsection 1 Variation of cell motive (m. 159–183)	4.1 Subsection 1 2– and 3 note cell motives are developed (m. 198–232)	5.1 Subsection 1 Fugue returns unison (m. 233–272)
1.2 Subsection 2 Violin joins fugue (m. 29–52) Tonal Center of D	2.2 Subsection 2 Violin and viola join cello (m. 129–158)	3.2 Subsection 2 Block chord texture (m. 184–198)		5.2 Subsection 2 Fugue theme devel–oped (m. 273–292)
1.3 Subsection 3 Cello enters with pizzacato figures based on cello motive (m. 53–96)				5.3 Subsection 3 3–note cell motive and block chord texture alternate with minor 3rd motive (m. 292–307)

at m. 96, where the linear elements of the three–note cell, tritone and minor third motive figure prominently in the 33–measure solo passage. These motives also provide the primary elements for a long development section which follows in all three instruments and leads directly to a new, strongly rhythmic section dominated by the linear triplet cell figures. These are executed by uniquely string bowing effects that provide a highly sonoristic character to the section (*tallone* and *sul* G and D). As a contrast to this predominantly linear texture the block chords return at measure 183. After 10 bars the harsh character of the section subsides into a triplet–dominated diminuendo that leads into the next section *poco meno mosso.* (Chart II)

Again string effects (*pizzacato, sul ponticello* and *con sordino*) and dramatic changes in dynamics provide the framework for "old friends": the *pizzacato* motive of the first *Adagio*, the minor third of the fugue theme, and the viola cell motive. This brilliantly conceived change of pace provides just the right release for the return, through a four measure accelerando, of the fugue theme and the reprise.

Whereas the main theme of Movement 2 was presented in contrapuntal style in its original appearance, Penderecki provides a totally new setting in the reprise (A1). Introduced quietly by the viola in the work's tonal center of G, the other instruments join four measures later in a 23–bar bravura unison statement of the theme that rises from piano to fortissimo until it breaks off into a short development passage at bar 258. The block chords return 10 bars later and lead to a coda–like two–part final section (*poco piu animato* and *agitato*) that begins with the fugue theme and introduces the motivic and rhythmic elements of the work one last time.

SINFONIETTA PER ARCHI

The overall form and texture of the *Sinfonietta* is similar to the *Trio*, but the addition of second violin and bass parts, as well as the extra instruments of the chamber orchestra, make the work somewhat less intimate. The score calls for 8 first violins, 6 seconds, 4 violas, 4 cellos and 1 double bass. Two other changes are recognizable when the score is closely studied: revised and additional metronome markings[7] and rehearsal numbers are added [these were absent in the score of the Trio]. The block chords that begin the work contain an added C natural in the double bass part which was not present in the original version [a and f are still absent]. It is interesting to note that Penderecki makes no other changes in the quadruple stops: the second violins double the chords of the first violins and the two viola parts are identical. The only revision is the addition of the double bass chord with the notes E D G C. In so far as the scoring of the chamber orchestra version is concerned, Penderecki creates 4 violin I parts (2 players on a part), 3 violin II parts (2 on a part), 2 viola

Ex. 7, Penderecki, *Sinfonietta*, scoring of cell motive, rehearsal 3

©1991 Schott Musik Internationale. Used by permission.

parts (2 on a part), 4 cello parts (1 player on a part) and 1 doublebass part in movement one. While in the second movement he sticks with the five parts (2 violins, viola, cello, bass) but writes divisi for violin I and II between rehearsal numbers 16 and 17. The additional instruments make the biggest difference in the texture of movement one. Instead of keeping the cell motive in one instrument, as he did in the Trio, Penderecki alternates it among the various instruments of the section (Ex. 7), thereby giving the motive a linear motion that provides more contrast than the earlier version. An interesting use of the cello and bass scoring is found in movement two at rehearsal number 9. In developing two of the basic motives of the movement, the minor third and cell motives, Penderecki brings a new timbre to the writing by alternating the material between doublebass and cello. (Ex. 8) One is reminded here of the way Mozart scores similar motives in the development sections of his symphonies and string quartets.

Ex. 8, Penderecki, *Sinfonietta*, scoring of basic motives, rehearsal 9

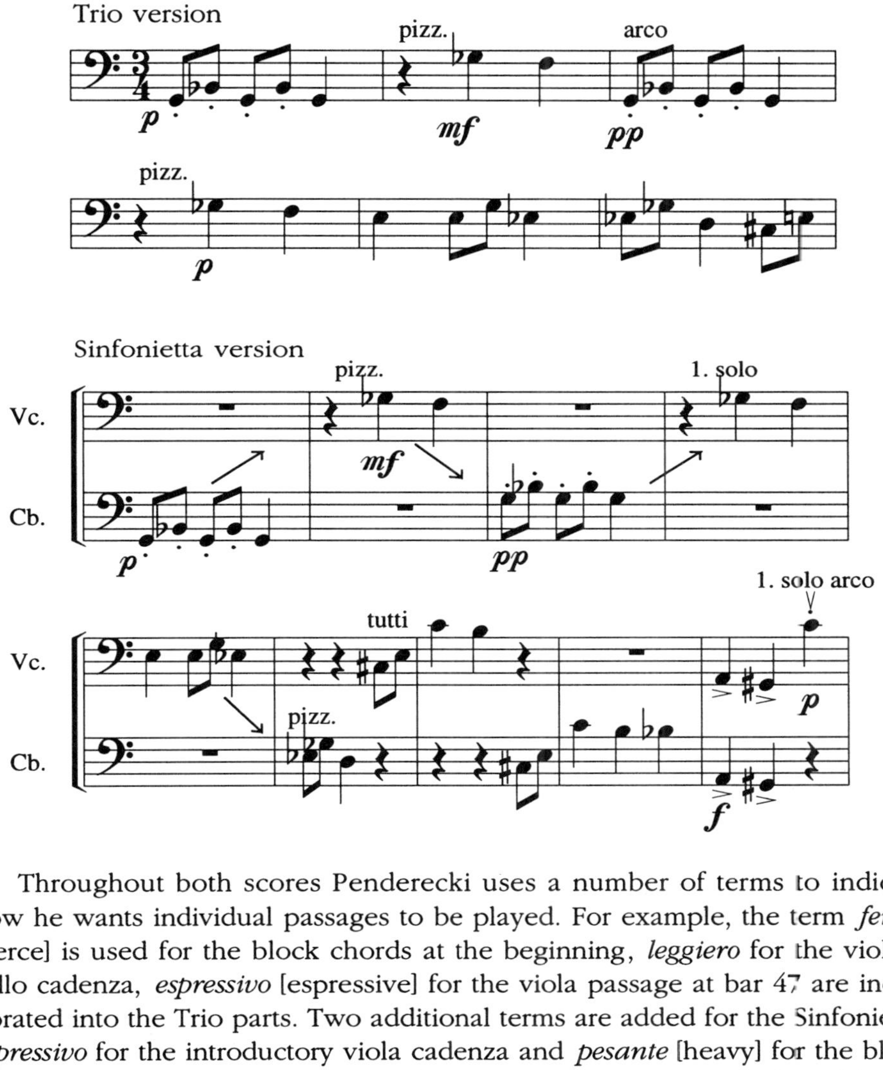

Throughout both scores Penderecki uses a number of terms to indicate how he wants individual passages to be played. For example, the term *feroce* [fierce] is used for the block chords at the beginning, *leggiero* for the violoncello cadenza, *espressivo* [espressive] for the viola passage at bar 47 are incorporated into the Trio parts. Two additional terms are added for the Sinfonietta: *espressivo* for the introductory viola cadenza and *pesante* [heavy] for the block chords at rehearsal numbers 5 and 13 in movement two. Penderecki uses these Italian terms to make it very clear how he wants these passages played, thus providing one further indication of the craftsmanship he brings to his art.

The String Trio and *Sinfonietta* are both significant additions to the repertory of the trio and chamber orchestra literature. They also confirm a new stylistic tendency in Penderecki's works that was first signalled by the opera

Ubu Rex. While many of the old devices are present, there is a conciseness of form and a clarity of intent here that brings to mind a style of an earlier era. There is little doubt that both works will soon become part of the standard repertory for their respective genre.

NOTES

1. The one exception is a short, but stylistically important, work for string quartet entitled *Der unterbrochene Gedanke,* composed in 1988.

2. Quoted in: Gerald Brennan, "A Rebel in Maturity. Ledgendary Polish Composer Krzysztof Penderecki at U.M.", *The Ann Arbor News,* March 8, 1995, p. C–4.

3. The "arch" is a form used by Belá Bartók in his Concerto for Orchestra and other works. Its main characteristics are the five sections (A–B–C–B–A) in which sections I and V and II and IV are related in musical content and the middle section (C) forms the center piece of the arch construction.

4. *Spiccato* and *sul ponticello* are color effects that are unique to string instruments. The former is a style of bowing played off the string, while the latter technique brings the bow close to the bridge and produces a kind of "whistling" sound.

5. For a thorough analysis of the musical materials in the *St. Luke Passion,* see: Ray Robinson and Allen Winold, *A Study of the Penderecki 'St. Luke Passion'* (Celle: Moeck Verlag, 1983) or the German edition *Die Lukaspassion von Krzysztof Penderecki* (Celle: Moeck Verlag, 1993)

6. *Arco battuto* and *tallone* are also string effects. The first means to strike the strings with the hair of the bow, while the latter refers to playing in the lower part of the bow (literally, at the nut of the bow.)

7. The first *Andante* (bar 3 of the introductory section) did not have a tempo marking in the Trio; in the *Sinfonietta* Penderecki adds the metronome marking ♪=70. The metronome marking at the first *Vivo,* rehearsal number 3, is changed from ♪=150 in the Trio to ♪=132 in the orchestral version.

Robert Shankovich

PITTSBURGH

Symphony No. 5 (Revised Version)

The first performance of Penderecki's *Symphony No. 5* took place in 1992 in Seoul, Korea, with the composer himself conducting the Seoul Philharmonic Orchestra. (The grand passacaglia which culminates the work uses thematic material drawn from a Korean folk melody.) The Pittsburgh performances, however, marked the world premiere of the revised version of the piece. Not much could be learned at the time about precisely what the composer had changed. But markings which had been added to certain orchestral parts suggest that at least some of the refinements were made by Penderecki the conductor. According to him, the same creative powers are at work in conducting as well as composing. At any rate, Maazel's re–creation of *"Penderecki's Fifth"* amply demonstrated to the public Penderecki's new level of artistic maturation—specifically his return to a neo–romantic style and his mastery of the symphonic form. Although a one–movement piece, the sections are clearly discernible. Moreover, listeners are left with no doubt about Penderecki's knowledge of the orchestra and the breadth of subtle expression of which its instruments are capable. Under his pen, instruments often relinquish their traditional roles within the orchestra; *e.g.*, the strings are not assigned, as ordinarily expected, to only "singing the tunes." Furthermore, Penderecki's sonic–spatial concepts are fascinating, as in this work which calls for a horn played off–stage, and four trumpeters stationed in the auditorium.

The success of the Pittsburgh performance can be gauged and indeed documented by synthesizing three points of view—that of the audience, the performers and the composer himself. Although the musical preferences of Western Pennsylvanians often seem to lean toward the conservative side, announcements of the Pittsburgh Symphony Orchestra's offering a Penderecki work generated a definite air of anticipation. Penderecki had long since made his mark on this region's devotees of serious music. Many associated him primarily with his early adventurous experiments with musical composition, and yet, despite any alleged conservatism, they crowded into Heinz Hall to hear this new work. Their response was overwhelmingly enthusiastic. In their newspaper reviews, the music critics praised both the music and the orchestra's performance of it. Secondly, the performer's point of view, gleaned from conversations with some of the orchestral musicians during the week of rehearsal of *Symphony No. 5*, and then again after the concert, was a unanimous expression of fascination with the music. "Every measure seemed ingratiating to play..." Third and perhaps most significant of all was the satisfaction expressed by the composer that his opus had been given a fair play—that his conception was faithfully rendered and his intention effectively communicated.

One can safely suppose that with this performance, Krzysztof Penderecki has made many new friends. Moreover, as this particular work gains familiarity, history may eventually have to be rewritten, relinquishing the top spot held for so long by that other composer whose name has been inextricably linked with "The Fifth Symphony."

Irina Nikolska

MOSCOW

Penderecki's *Utrenya* in Moscow

Utrenya (1969–71) was performed in the Grand Hall of the Moscow Conservatory on 18 May 1995 by the State Orchestra conducted by Vladimir Ponkin. The performers were the "Russian Music" Foundation Choir (Valeri Maksimov, Choirmaster), the boy's choir from the town of Konakovo (prepared by Vadim Mahnovski), soloists Ewa Irzykowska, Vita Nikolaienko, Piotr Kusiewicz, Radosław Łukowski (from Poland) and Georgiy Ter–Margarian. Krzysztof Penderecki was present at the concert and conducted the Song of Cherubim (1986) for a cappella choir, which, as *Utrenya*, draws from the tradition of Orthodox music.

Without doubt the concert was a success, the audience welcome was very warm although perhaps not as enthusiastic as it might have been a decade or so ago. The reasons for this circumstance include the overall decrease of interest in contemporary music, as well as the apparent crisis situation on various levels of Russian culture. *Utrenya* had come into being over a quarter of a century earlier [Part I in 1970; Part II, 1971], but this concert marked the first time the work was performed in an Orthodox country. In recent years a great number of works based on the Orthodox liturgy have been written in Russia. *Utrenya*, however, does not have anything to do with Russian music. It is very far from the canon of Orthodox Church tradition, which required music to be written solely for a cappella choir. In Penderecki's work an important role is played by the orchestra. There are references to church songs and even quotations from the Easter liturgy, which are combined in an interesting way with sonoristic means. The whole work creates an expressive sound aura, in which the solemn procession finds its reflection from Entombment to the triumph of the Resurrection.

Responding to questions at the press conference and at the meeting with Russian listeners, which dealt mainly with his interpretation of liturgical orthodoxy, Penderecki stressed a number of basic facts. He became interested in Orthodox music in his child–hood years when his father (born in Stanisławów, currently the Ukrainian town Ivano–Frankovsk) often told him about Orthodox liturgy. Yet, he did not see any influence of professional Orthodox church music (Bortniansky, Tchaikovsky, Rachmaninov and others) in *Utrenya*. His inspiration was primarily drawn from the Orthodox music of Southeastern Europe (Yugoslavia, Bulgaria). The Soviet authorities were not very happy about the composer's attempts to become familiar with Orthodox culture, and after he had written *Utrenya*, every consecutive Soviet Minister of Culture promised him that they would organize the first performance [in the Soviet Union], which they failed to put into practice. They always found a convenient reason to refuse. Using the opportunity of the Russian premiere, the press revealed that the (unoffficial) ban on *Utrenya* had been caused by the fact that its score was a combination of Orthodoxy and the avant garde. "This had been definitely too much for one work." (*Sewodnia* [Today] newspaper, No. 93, 25 May 1995).

The most convincing moment for the Russian recipient of *Utrenya* was its emotional content, which was due to the composer's excellent grasp of Orthodox religious experience. The theatrical elements were highlighted as well. The well–known director of the Bolshoi Theater in Moscow, Boris Pokrovsky, when asked about his impressions after the first performance of *Utrenya*, said: "I could see it." In one of the reviews the identity of the work's basic humanistic message for all the people in the world was rightly stressed and it was compared with Alexander Skryabin's long contemplated and ultimately unfinished "Mysterium." Other reviews pointed out the political context: if in the 1960's the *Passion according to St. Luke* was as if a condensation of resistance against Communist lies and atheism in Poland, then in the 1970's the return to Orthodox symbolism was motivated by the resistance against the totalitarian "Big Brother who fought against the icons" (*Sewodnia*, 25 May 1995).

The performance itself was not ideal. Fortunately the greatness of *Utrenya* "was able to speak for itself." The Polish soloists did the best job. The basso–profondo, the Russian Georgiy Ter–Margarian, delighted the audience neither with his voice nor with his artistic ability. Besides, one could feel that the choir had difficulty performing this kind of music since it lacked experience in performing modern music in general, hence its timidity, uncertainty and lack of precision in joining the orchestra. The latter turned out to perform much better than the choir singers.

The performance of *Utrenya* in Moscow was an event of such magnitude in Russian musical life that it is hardly possible to spoil it with remarks of performance deficiencies. The return of Penderecki to Russia after an interval of nine years, and the excitement it brought about in musical circles, prove what a profound bond links the Russian audiences with the Maestro's music. The recordings of his music are still best–sellers and every concert of Penderecki's turns into a grand event in the cultural life of Russia.

Allen Winold

BLOOMINGTON, INDIANA

Penderecki's Violin Concerto No. 2: World Premiere

Res severa verum gaudium

This Latin quotation, inscribed on a banner at the rear of the stage of the famed *Gewandhaus* hall in Leipzig, was especially appropriate for the world premiere of the *Concerto No. 2 for Violin and Orchestra* of Krzysztof Penderecki, played in this magnificent hall on June 24, 1995 by the renowned German violinist Anne–Sophie Mutter and the Symphony Orchestra of the Middle German Radio under the direction of Mariss Jansons.

Res severa verum gaudium—a serious thing (brings) true joy—could serve as a motto for Penderecki's works in general and for this work in particular. Penderecki is one of the most serious and dedicated composers of our time, and this work is highly serious and demanding in length, complexity and emotional scope. However, it certainly brought true joy as evidenced by the rapt attention the Leipzig public gave it throughout the performance and the tumultuous applause and standing ovations they gave it at the end of the performance.

The concerto was commissioned by the Middle German Radio and the premiere performance was the festive opening concert of the fourth annual "Music Summer", a series of concerts in the three German states served by the Middle German Radio — Thüringen, Sachsen, and Sachsen–Anhalt. The work is dedicated to the soloist, Anne–Sophie Mutter. The first concerto written some twenty years earlier was dedicated to Isaac Stern.

The concerto is written in a single movement and evokes memories of other single–movement large–scale works, including the composer's own first concerto. On first hearing the second concerto strikes the listener as an extremely convincing blend of tradition and innovation and a highly effective balance of unity and variety. Traditional aspects range from evocations of the materials and techniques of the violin concertos of Brahms, Tchaikovski, and others to references to compositional techniques and structures in the works of Bartók, Debussy, Strauß and others. Especially in the second half of the work there seems to be conscious reference to traditional forms and types — scherzos, dances, song–like passages, humorous passages, virtuoso display passages including a lengthy and prodigiously demanding solo cadenza, and the marvelous elegiac section at the close of the work. The first part of the work, by contrast, seems to be devoted more to abstract exploration of thematic and technical possibilities. Despite the obvious surface variety present in the work, one can sense and at times can clearly identify the use of a limited set of musical materials in the work which lends it a strong sense of musical unity.

Like Joachim for the Brahms violin concerto or David for the Mendelssohn violin concerto, Anne–Sophie Mutter was not only the first performer for Penderecki's second violin concerto but also the ideal interpreter for the work. She brought all the necessary requisites to the performance — a violinistic technique that is so secure that one never even thinks about it during the performance, a variety of tone colors ranging from rich intensity to etheric clarity with all shadings in between, a sense of rhythm and phrasing that makes every passage clear and convincing and incidentally makes the difficult task of the conductor much easier, and an understanding of the work that made her a true co–creator. More than this, Mutter brought to this performance a sense of total dedication and commitment. The work is enormously demanding for the soloist, not only in terms of the difficulty of the many passages, but also in terms of the sheer length of the work and the fact that the solo violin plays almost constantly throughout.

Mariss Jansons and the Middle German Radio Orchestra more than met the challenges of this difficult score. In many sections it is a "concerto for orchestra with violin" and the solo and tutti players of the ensemble played with great effectiveness. The conductor and orchestra also provided a marvelous frame for the concerto with a spirited performance of Rossini's Overture to *The Italian Girl in Algiers* and a disciplined but expressive reading of the Brahms *Symphony No. 1.* The entire concert was repeated on June 26 in the famed *Semper Oper* of Dresden with the same participants and with the same successful reaction from the public.

In today's musical life it is unforunately rare that performances of new works are truly memorable experiences. However, for the premiere performance of this concerto the constellation of a superb soloist, a splendid orcehstra, a brilliant conductor, a knowledgeable and enthusiastic public, a marvelous auditorium with unbelievable good acoustics, and above all a work that clearly deserves a place among the masterworks of this century, made this a truly memorable event.

Marek Stachowski

CRACOW

Penderecki's Violin Concerto No. 2: Polish Premiere in Katowice

The world premiere of Krzysztof Penderecki's *Violin Concerto No. 2* took place on June 24, 1995, in Leipzig, Germany. Anne–Sophie Mutter, to whom the Concerto is dedicated, appeared as soloist and the Middle German Radio Orchestra was conducted by Mariss Jansons. The Polish premiere took place on December 21, 1995, in the Silesian city of Katowice, and featured the American violinist Alyssa Park and the Polish Radio National Symphony Orchestra under the direction of the composer. This review is directed to the Polish performance.

Penderecki composed the Concerto during the years 1992–95. The work reflects a metamorphosis in the composer's career, which the eminent Polish musicologist Mieczysław Tomaszewski labelled as a "period of new synthesis".[1] Other compositions which reflect this period of personal evolution in Penderecki's work include the "Sanctus" from the *Polish Requiem*, "Benedictus" for a cappella choir and the *Quartet for Clarinet and String Trio.*

Specifically, this period of new synthesis displays two essential pecularities in Penderecki's work. These pecularities, or values, are manifested in his exploitation of extremely different musical formal structures, and the musical material which operates within these structures. Secondly, taking into account Penderecki's compositions previous to the Concerto (*Ubu Rex*, *Symphony No. 5* "Korean", *Sinfonietta per Archi)*, there exists the notion in his philosophical belief that the composer lives and acts within the decline of the twentieth century and the second millenium. Penderecki has emphasized the necessity to fulfill the task of an essential synthesis in art, which would be the metaphysical answer to the "acute pain, and feeling of the disintegration of the world."[2]

After the *St. Luke Passion* was composed in 1966, there were the beginning steps of this new synthesis in his work. The musical language of the compositions written in the last several years exhibit a striving to create a universal musical language. According to Penderecki, this personal and universal notion "enables [me] in a natural way to write music in accordance to my feeling."[3] Since the composition of the *Passion*, these personal compositional requirements are evident up to his most recent works.

The *Violin Concerto No. 2* belongs to the group of compositions in which Penderecki decisively fulfills the quest of synthesizing and universalizing his musical language. The Concerto displays a new and idiomatic method which may be categorized into the areas of expression, and the strong dramaturgy of form, or musical architecture. Both of these areas are intrinsic to Penderecki's later works, and this new synthesized approach is most evident and concrete in the second violin concerto.

Considering Penderecki's formal design in the Concerto, the work is a continuation of a principle he developed in the 1980's. Here, there occurs continuous alterations of initial pitch material, micro–structures or cells, and gestures including orchestral temporal acoustic possibilities. These elements in various combinations take place within the overall formal layout of the Concerto. Further, the micro–structure, which mainly consists of chromatic steps, minor seconds, minor thirds and tritones are important in the hierarchy of intervals since these intervals determine the elementary thematic material of the work. Penderecki concisely introduces this intervallic hierarchy in the opening bars of the composition, along with a complete exposition of themes and micro–structural cells. Up until [rehearsal number 5] in the score, these consist of:

- juxtapositions of rising four note chromatic structures;
- steady half notes introduced in violin I and violin II;
- longer musical ideas, resulting from combinations of the above mentioned structural cells.

The essential elements of musical material are introduced by the solo violin within a wide spread of sound spectrum from low key timbre up to A4. The violin solo of this section presents all the important and essential combinations of the basic motivic elements, except the tritone. However, the tritone appears intervallically between the notes of the solo violin and the counterpointing micro–thematic structures of the string section of the orchestra.

The Concerto is a one–movement work, in which the first section of the composition (m. 1–36) proceeds in four phases. The first and last phrase construct a formal framework. The two internal phrases contain musical material exposed in the first measures of the work and which subsequently undergo intense variation and stratification. A short link or bridge section, resembling a counter–part to the middle section, which is similar in formal outlook to the middle movement of a classic period concerto. Also, a new synthetic pattern appears, which consists of successive variations and micro–structural alterations. For example, in the closing phase of the section at [58], the tempo is strengthened by strong triplet motion. These echo–like triplet gestures, or explored orchestral acoustic temporal possibilities, are a highly characteristic feature of Penderecki's recent compositions.

The last section of the Concerto (from [67] to the end) also proceeds in four phases. This alludes to the final movement of a classic period concerto, and the work ends with the note D spread in seven octaves throughout the orchestral tutti. However, an A appears in the first oboe a subtle recapitulation to the A pitch center of the beginning of the work.

The score of the *Violin Concerto No. 2* shows Krzysztof Penderecki as a composer conscious of the necessity to synthesize and further the entire Western musical tradition. All of his compositions written after 1985 bear the seal of a composer's struggle with the enigma of a creator to observe everything composed in the history of Western music. The *Violin Concerto No. 2* is a representative work acknowledging the composer's conviction that "one can not do everything from the beginning. One can only continue".[4]

The Polish premiere of the Concerto produced an exceptionally subtle performance displaying brilliant virtuosity as well as great sensitivity and elegance. Alyssa Park revealed a wide spectrum of delicate idiomatic timbre combined with precision and excellent violin technique. Her performance de–monstrated a sound interpretation and understanding of the score. The composer, who conducted the Polish premiere, allowed the music to flow evenly. Typical of the composer's music, a strong sense of drama was built by conducting the compositional components with a "breathing" expression of the score, a characteristic typical of Penderecki's conducting technique. Excellent control of orchestral dynamics, observances of important linear structures, and overall balance between soloist and orchestra were executed with solid leadership and intelligence.

Notes

1. See Mieczysław Tomaszewski, *Krzysztof Penderecki i jego muzyka* [Krzysztof Penderecki and his music], (Kraków: Akademia Muzyczna, 1994)

2. See the interview with the composer in *Dekada Literacka* [Literary Decade] 1:1–2 (June 1992).

3. See Penderecki's interview entitled "Muzyki nie można zaczynać od początku" ["In music one cannot start from the beginning"], *Ruch Muzyczny 22* (1987), p. 9.

4. Penderecki, "Interview," *ibid.*

Robert Shankovich

PITTSBURGH

Performing Krzysztof Penderecki's *Passio et Mors domini Nostri Jesu Christi Secundum Lucam*: A Conductor's Preparation

(DMA dissertation by Wes Janzen, University of Cincinnati, 1994.)

As one of the requirements for his degree in Choral Conducting Performance, Janzen offers this thorough and comprehensive study of Penderecki's monumental work, *The Passion and death of Our Lord Jesus Christ according to St. Luke*. It is directed to conductors seeking "a serious performance of the Passion." (Could any performance of this work conceivably be otherwise?) The author pinpoints and addresses the many interpretive problems which will inevitably be encountered in the course of score study and subsequent rehearsals—errata, performance practice, Penderecki's latest revisions of the score, *et. al.* Janzen is well qualified for the task; his information has been gleaned directly from primary sources—considerable time spent with Penderecki, free access to the composer's sketches and all other editions and versions of the score and parts, as well as "many hours of insightful discussions" with American chorus master Dale Warland during Warland's preparation of the choruses for performances of the *St. Luke Passion* at the 1990 Oregon Bach Festival (which Penderecki conducted). Janzen covers his topic in six chapters ending with as many pages of Bibliography—probably of secondary importance considering that most of the entries date from the 1960s.

As every conductor knows, adequate "score preparation" is an essential prerequisite to approaching the rehearsal podium. The process inevitably involves musical analysis—the mode of which is dictated by the type and complexity of the music. Conductors choose the analytical approach with which they are most conversant, and which they believe will yield for them the most profound understanding of the musical work. Janzen asserts that he is not proffering any analysis, nor does he promise any "comprehensive interpretive guide." His stated objective is to encourage more conductors to consider the programming of this composition, having provided them with information which will ensure an interpretation adhering more closely to Penderecki's intention beyond what can be, or has been encoded in the score. This is precisely what is chronicled in chapters three and four of Janzen's study, titled respectively, "Part I of the Score," and "Part II of the Score," described later in this review.

Chapter One, "Four Stages of Composition and a Description of Sources," chronicles the evolution of the *St. Luke Passion* from the composer's first sketches ("hundreds" of them, now stored in his Cracow home) to the final autograph full score (housed at WDR [West German Radio] in Cologne from which the orchestra parts were published). The version of the fourth stage does not yet exist. It is to consist of a final revision of the score, purged of notational errors, and containing more explicit instructions regarding performance practice based on Penderecki's latest changes of mind concerning certain passages throughout the work. This is curious considering the number of successful performances of this work already given. (Many Penderecki scholars contend that it was the *St. Luke Passion* that catapulted the composer to world fame.) The reckoning of "four stages" is Penderecki's own: but whether the fourth–stage version of this already thirty–year–old composition will ever materialize seems doubtful. Even though the composer acknowledges the urgent need for it, the project may be destined to remain simmering on the back burner, while he attends to the more immediate demands on his time and artistry.

The proliferation of problems with the score is explained in part by the number of sources (eleven in all!) consulted by Janzen in the course of his research, and the discrepancies within and among these sources. The word "sources" refers here to extant forms of the music—sketches, holographs, and versions or editions of the complete work, or portions of it which came into being during the first three stages of composition. Some are available for purchase: the full score co–published by Polskie Wydawnictwo Muzyczne (Poland) and Moeck Verlag (Germany); the miniature full score Moeck No. 5028—the score with pagination referred to by Janzen in his dissertation. Some other sources are available through rental, and still others are stored in archives, or are personal property accessible only by special arrangement. The dates written on some of these sources are enigmatic, and Janzen has attempted to unscramble some of the confusion about chronology. But whether or not his reckoning is totally accurate remains a subject for debate among other Penderecki scholars with whom he takes exception.

Penderecki worked on different parts of the *St. Luke Passion* at different times. The problem of chronology turns out to be a symptom rather than the malady, however. For example, our evolved system of traditional notation has managed to survive its built–in inadequacies, that is, until now. Performers who strive for accuracy of rendition temper fidelity to the score with historical research of performance practice. But the "new sounds" of modern music necessitated new notation, and precipitated additional questions for the performer. Penderecki has been heard by this reviewer to say he invented graphic notation, but Janzen quotes him as definitely attributing it to a professor at the Academy of Music in Cracow. Nevertheless, Penderecki adapted some elements of it in scoring the *St. Luke Passion.* Publishers, confronted with unfamiliar symbols, were prone to error. Added to this is the known fact that Penderecki was often late in submitting his manuscripts to the publishers causing them to work in haste, compounding the possibilities of mistakes in the printed score ("hundreds of them"). But the problem is even more complicated. From Janzen's conversations with Penderecki, we learn that over the years the composer has changed his mind about several interpretative matters concerning this piece; we can safely infer that he may still be undecided about some things. Janzen explains, "This is part of his [Penderecki's] wonderful personality."

Much of the controversy is over the aleatoric passages in the *St. Luke Passion.* Penderecki does not wish his score to be too exacting or overly restrictive. He has thus risked trusting the conductor/performer to make the "right" choices. However, the probability of spending the necessary time researching, and rehearsal time in experimentation to get it "right" is highly unlikely; and so it has been. It should be noted that Penderecki himself is a consummate conductor. He has told this reviewer that conducting enables him to add to the music those interpretative nuances which, for any number of reasons, were not, or could not be written into the score by the composer. He seems to penetrate the psyche of the composer, and, reading between the lines of the score imbues the composition with unique freshness. This explains why, in his own conducting of his own piece, Penderecki is able to achieve what he wants. No one else can be expected to do that! (Penderecki has his own conducting score which he has annotated, along with a set of orchestral parts reserved for his exclusive use.)

In his chapter two, "An Overview of the Work," Janzen merely gives a general description of the piece similar to what one reads in the notes of a record jacket. Chapter five provides an account of Dale Warland's chorus rehearsals, followed by Penderecki's full rehearsals in preparation for the Oregon Bach Festival performances of the *Passion.* But it is the third and fourth chapters mentioned above, taking up about 160 pages of Janzen's 212–page dissertation, that provide the most important substance of the work. It is a measure–by–measure compendium of "corrections, revisions, clarifications, solutions to problems, and interpretative instructions" collected by the author. Very interesting and perhaps most valuable are Penderecki's own words which Janzen has painstakingly kept intact and in context. The paragraph quoted here from page 95 is a good example:

> At present, only the composer is able to give clear and adequate performance information to the conductor wishing to prepare the work. The published material is not enough. It leaves too many questions unanswered. This is not efficient. In discussing

> these problems, and specifically page 44, the composer affirmed my research by saying, "You know this work better than anyone. You know exactly how it was [in the original manuscripts], and maybe how it's going to be [with a new edition], I, [Penderecki] don't even know." He added, "There are so many mistakes, and then, also so many question marks, even for me." He indicated that for a revision he will want to work from the original manuscripts. "I [Penderecki] have done this piece so many times [conducted so many performances] and I don't remember everything [past manuscripts, performances, changes]."

Page 44 in the above quote refers go the Moeck edition, No. 5028, which is necessary for following Janzen's narrative.

Some brief comment concerning Janzen's "thesis" as he calls it (actually by strict definition, a dissertation): The author is inconsistent in literary style in his mixed usage of the first and third person. There are occasional typographical errors or misspelled words, including the absence of the diacritical marks required for correct spelling of certain Polish words. Finally Janzen has unintentionally created some humorous imagery—*e.g.*, on page 42, "...the choir should not sit in bar 2...." Fortunately none of this blemishes the integrity of the work. By virtue of his exhaustive study of Penderecki's *St. Luke Passion*, he has, in a very practical sense established himself as the co–creator of this great musical work. He has, as Penderecki says, learned more about the piece than anyone else, and in that sense his research has been fruitful. But whether conductors will be persuaded to, or dissuaded from performing Penderecki's *Passion* as a result of reading Janzen's paper can, at this point, only be conjectured.

Maria Piotrowska

WARSAW

Krzysztof Penderecki i jego muzyka. Cztery eseje

In the book by Mieczysław Tomaszewski entitled *Krzysztof Penderecki i jego muzyka. Cztery eseje* (*Krzysztof Penderecki and his Music: Four Essays*),[1] the nature of Penderecki's music has found an excellent rendering, both in its entire scope and in the minute detail. The book is an example of the synthesis which does not stray in the slightest from the firm ground of good analysis, the natural purpose and use of which is to serve interpretation and make it believable. The object of Tomaszewski's essays is, in the final account, the Eggebrecht's unity, the *Sinngehalt* [essence], of Penderecki's music, approached in the book from various ranges and in different approximations. But Tomaszewski is also a careful historian, that is why he has found room for the chronology of Penderecki's life and work, including the division of his work into periods, as well as for a sizeable (1/3 of the book) Appendix, containing *e.g.* the list of Penderecki's works, bibliography of the Polish sources, and even brief notes on the academic sessions which have been organized in Poland to honor Krzysztof Penderecki.

As the author himself notes in the Afterword, each of the four parts of the book is of a different nature since they came into being separately and at different times (1986, 1991, 1993); there is something that makes them similar, however, and this is the author's personal attitude to the subject. The attitude leaves no doubt as to its nature, and yet it is a factor deeply hidden in the book, which has only inspired the author rather than making his analyses subjective.

The first essay is entitled *Słuchając Pendereckiego* [Listening to Penderecki]; in this way the author signalizes the priority given to direct understanding, the phenomenological insight into sound processes of incredibly high evocative power, which can be broken into: "spontaneity, lavishness, vitality, energy release, a dynamic chain of sound events, the operating of primary factors" (p. 9)[2]. From the very beginning the author keeps stressing the most striking feature of the music—its unique completeness both in the area of material and the means employed; the latter include those rooted in the sonoristic conceptions of the avant–garde as well as the language elements of "all significant historical styles and techniques of the last millenium." This excess, however, subjected to "the high temperature of creativeness" (p. 10) melts into a smooth alloy of individual poetics. The composer's repertoire of means, painstakingly developed and then mastered as if it were a living language, acquires the appropriate meaning in the service of the content, with which it is in deep and full accord. In the sphere of content, the importance of religious themes is another striking feature; they are drawn principally from the Old and the New Testaments, but at the same time they are strongly linked to broader philosophical and moral issues, depending on the message of a given work.

In Tomaszewski's view, it is from both of these perspectives that Penderecki considers the puzzle of human existence, seeking its solution mainly in borderline situations (sin, suffering, death). These grand, universal themes are highly emotionally charged, and yet, as Tomaszewski points out, in Penderecki's work this emotion does not assume a personal shape; it is rather a quasi–Baroque "expressive theatre," in which "a convention takes precedence over the directness of expression, the theatrical suspension of disbelief over psychological or realistic truth" (p. 13). The spread of desemantization techniques, which have consistently been applied to words, makes the culminations of Penderecki's works all the more significant; they contain quotations, made more lucid for the occasion, which carry key messages and lend the "meaningful form" character to the works. This is not to say that the playful element, which evokes pure games with the sound, does not have its role in the meaningful reality too.

In the second essay, *Słowo i dźwięk w muzyce Pendereckiego* (Word and Sound in Penderecki's Music), Tomaszewski discusses the correlation between word and sound in a more detailed fashion than in the first essay, simultaneously introducing the reader into the problem of the evolution of Penderecki's work. It turns out that the whole notional and artistic program of his music, taking place, to use Tomaszewski's words, "within the short–circuit, at the hot edge of the sacred and the profane" (p. 21), was already present in the composer's earliest works written in the years 1958–60. Their ground–breaking character has been confirmed in his later work by the following factors: individual attitude to each text (reductions, interpolations); anchoring "eternal" themes in current meaning; systematic expansion of the range of material and the repertoire of technical means, which has led to the works becoming monumental; finally, growing control over the form, apparent in the development of his artistic principles. While the poetics of Penderecki's earlier works could be described, in Tomaszewski's view, in terms of such notions as "assembly", "dissipation", "clash", "permutation", or "combinatorial analysis", his later works are better characterized by the notions of "evolution," "gradation," "transformation," "culmination," "reprise," etc., and the role of the playful element diminishes there. According to Tomaszewski, this proves that "the poetics of the suite [has given in to] the poetics of the sonata" (p. 27), and that the dramaturgy of

Penderecki's works (or "synthetic" dramaturgy in the case of works containing text) has taken a mature shape. The development is accompanied by the growing "cohesion of musical text." The level reached by individual works brings them into a dialogue of sorts with the grand achievements of past composers. And here, Tomaszewski juxtaposes *St. Luke's Passion* and that of Bach's *St. Matthew Passion*, *Utrenya* and *Glagolithic Mass*, *The Devils of Loudun* and *Joan of Arc at the Stake*, the *Polish Requiem* and the requiems by Mozart and Brahms. In the course of brilliant analyses the author reveals a genuine universalism of Penderecki's music, written "in the time when the Tower of Babel has come to pass" (p. 40).

From the two other essays, the one which bears the title "Absorb all that has come to be" (the composer's artistic motto) deserves particular attention. The other essay (the last in the book) comprises only the biographical outline mentioned above as well as the presentation of subsequent phases in Penderecki's *oeuvre*, announced by the dominating motto–like titles of his key works. The third essay once again raises the problem of the composer employing the musical substance of past epochs, but here the author proposes an interesting classification of (not always novel) compositional means used in the process. Tomaszewski distinguishes three major principles:

1. *Cantus prius factus in cantum novum insertus*, music within music: includes "reminiscenses" (fleeting, vague suggestions of earlier style) and "quotations", allusive or unequivocal;
2. *Cantus secundum cantum*, music according to music: the category includes "stylized" music, in which, as the name suggests, the historical model is quite tangible, as well as "retroversive" music, "turned back, and yet no doubt personal, his own, experienced, deprived of the stylized quotation" (p. 75);
3. *Cantus novus de cantu omnigeno compositus*, music beyond music: works classified here draw from various stylistic idioms, "from fragments, bits and pieces of various origin" (p. 79), and the degree of their integration determines the distinctiveness of the proposed categories of "eclectic" and "synthetic" music. The attribution to Penderecki's music of the status of "speech," in which the ancient laws of rhetorical logic have not been invalidated and in which traditional, although suitably updated, rhetorical figures abound, completes the description of the composer's *oeuvre*; nothing else matches its greatness, it "speaks" suggestively and straghtforwardly even to antagonists of contemporary music, who are said to long for order and hierarchy. The acceptance seems to be largely due to the semiotic character of the music and to the key messages it conveys, particularly the strongest message of all—the message of hope. They draw their actual power from masterfully

> personified and, in the final account, musically independent "sound speech" units—this is the mystery revealed to us by Four Essays, the book highly erudite but also strong on intuition and sensitivity. The technical formulas of musicological language easily merge there into the discourse proper to humanities "which understand."

Thanks to Mieczysław Tomaszewski's mastery of the literary word, the mindboggling complexity of Krzysztof Penderecki's mastery of sound has found its faithful reflection.

NOTES

1. Mieczysław Tomaszewski, *Krzysztof Penderecki i jego muzyka. Cztery eseje* [*Krzysztof Penderecki and his Music: Four Essays*] (Kraków: Akademia Muzyczna, 1994).

2. The numbers in parenthesiss refer to page numbers in the book reviewed.

Translated by Władysław Grzegorz Chłopicki

Ray Robinson

WEST PALM BEACH

Unpublished Research on Penderecki's Music by Scholars from American and Canadian Universities[1]

The music of Krzysztof Penderecki (b. 1933) has been an extremely popular topic for research in American universities during the last three decades of the twentieth century. Graduate students in the United States and Canada have selected Penderecki as the subject of their theses and dissertations nineteen times in the period 1970 to 1996. It is not just coincidental that this interest in the composer occurred following the early performances of his works in the United States. With the world premieres of the *String Quartet No. 1* (1962) in Cincinnati and the *Pittsburgh Overture* (1967) in Pittsburgh, and the first American performances of the *Capriccio for Violin* (1968) in Buffalo and the *St. Luke Passion* (1969) in San Francisco, St. Paul, and New York, it was obvious to scholars in the New World that Penderecki was a composer whose music was worthy of study. Additional American premieres in 1969 only added to the fascination with this new musical voice from Eastern Europe. There were six first performances in that year alone: *Threnody* in Philadelphia, *St. Luke* in San Francisco, *Dies Irae* in Louisville, *Sonata for Violoncello and Orchestra* and *Capriccio for Siegfried Palm* at the Dartmouth Festival in Hanover, New Hampshire, the *Devils of Loudun* in Santa Fe. It is therefore not surprising that the first American study on the composer (1970) sought to explore the stylistic elements in three of these works: *Threnody*, *St. Luke* and *Dies Irae*.

Gebuhr, Ann Karen: "Stylistic elements in selected works of Krzysztof Penderecki," MA thesis, Music Theory, Indiana University, Bloomington, Indiana, 1970, 139 pages, musical examples

The earliest American study on the music of Penderecki was completed in 1970 at Indiana University, one of the outstanding university schools of music in the United States. A masters thesis in the field of music theory, this study presents analyses of three of the composer's better known works from the decade of the 1960s: *Threnody to the Victims of Hiroshima* (1960), *The Passion and Death of Our Lord Jesus Christ according to Saint Luke* (1965–66) and *Dies Irae* (1967). The author has defined a dual purpose for the study; the first being an in–depth theoretical analysis of the three selected works. The works are approached through an analysis of linear events, rhythmic characteristics, vertical sonorities (including timbre and texture), and form. The second purpose is to identify those stylistic characteristics that are consistent in all three works and which describe the style used by Penderecki during the years 1959 to 1967. The final chapter contains a summary and listing of these characteristics.

Tyra, Thomas N.: "The analysis of three twentieth century compositions for wind ensemble," Ph.D dissertation, University of Michigan, Ann Arbor, Michigan, 1971, 223 pages, musical examples

The first doctoral dissertation on Penderecki's music to emerge from an American university was completed in 1971 and focused on the composer's *Pittsburgh Overture* (1967). Completed at the University of Michigan, it presents an analytical study of three twentieth century compositions for wind ensemble: *Symphonies of Wind Instruments* by Igor Stravinsky; *Octandre* by Edgard Varèse; and *Pittsburgh Overture* by Krzysztof Penderecki. The purpose of the study is two–fold: first, to make available to conductor–teachers careful analyses of these works along with discussions of the performance problems inherent in the music; and second, to provide models and analytical tools which may be useful in dealing with other contemporary compositions from the wind ensemble repertory.

The analysis of the *Pittsburgh Overture* (1967) centers around the serial procedures used in pitch control and the use of non–traditional notational devices, the latter stemming, in part, from the work's unmetered rhythmic style and its reliance on improvisation by the performers. Examination is made of the performance problems as they relate to the temporal progress of the music and to the control of improvised material. The formal structure of this single–movement work is discussed with special emphasis given to cadence patterns and methods of sectional overlap.

Linthicum, David Howell: "Penderecki's Notation: A critical evaluation," DMA dissertation, composition, University of Illinois, Urbana–Champaign, Illinois, 1972, 75 pages, music notation and paleography

This doctoral thesis attempts to define and clarify Penderecki's intentions as they relate to his use of notation in the sonoristic works of the 1960s. After placing the composer in historical perspective by surveying the background of aleatory thought and the development of the compositional aesthetic of the modern Polish school, the author draws certain conclusions as to the degree of success Penderecki has achieved in solving the problems inherent in notating a controlled aleatory situation in works composed between 1958 and 1967. The scope of the study is further limited to works written for conventional instruments and/or voices. In general, the discussion refers to those notational symbols which raise questions relating to clarity of intent and interpretation.

Kovalenko, Susan Chaffins: "The Twentieth Century Requiem: An emerging concept," Ph.D Washington University, St. Louis, Missouri, 1971, 336 pages, musical examples

The main objective of this study is to examine the many non–liturgical and frequently non–religious requiems written since the beginning of the twentieth century, and to account for these compositions as essentially modern phenomena with, however, extensive roots in previous eras. A brief survey of the Requiem Mass prior to the nineteenth century is given, and several Protestant funeral works with unique texts are studied as examples of early requiem–like compositions outside the framework of the Catholic liturgy. Various factors contributing to the development of the secular requiem are then explored. In an attempt to place today's requiem in context, a summary of modern attitudes toward death is given. It is shown that the two great wars of this century have had a profound effect upon present–day concepts of death, and that, in fact, the most important contemporary requiems deal not only with death, but are also deeply concerned with the problems and morality of war. For detailed examination, five large–scale, oratorio–like requiems of the twentieth century, all dealing in some way with war, are chosen: Frederick Delius', *Requiem* (1914–1916); Edward Elgar's, *The Spirit of England* (1919); Paul Hindemith's, *When Lilacs Last in the Doorway Bloom'd* (1946); Dimitri Kabalevsky's, *Requiem* (1963); and Krzysztof Penderecki's *Dies irae* (1967). Both texts and music of these widely differing works are analyzed at length, and comparisons are drawn between the ways in which the composers approach the subjects of war and death. It is concluded that the traditional concept of a requiem as a prayer for the rest of departed souls has been largely abandoned in the twentieth century and the form is in the process of becoming an important new musical genre—one which may concern itself not only with death, but with social and moral problems as well.

Gallaher, Christopher S.: "Density in Twentieth–Century Music" PhD, Theory, Indiana University, Bloomington, Indiana, 1975, 164 pages, musical examples

The primary purposes of this study are to determine the relative degrees of vertical and horizontal density in selected contemporary works and to ascertain how these changing patterns of density interact. Vertical density is defined in this study as the number, amplitude, registration and color (timbre) of sound events articulated in any given time segment (e.g. per measure or per second) while horizontal density is defined as the frequency (repetition) of occurrences of successive articulations.

More specifically, this investigation explores the possible relationships between the passage of time and events in new music and the subsequent creation of structural goals based on these relationships. The literature selected for this study includes: Earle Brown's *Holograph I* (1959); Lukas Foss', *Time Cycle* (1960); György Ligeti's, *Nouvelles Aventures* (1965); Krzysztof Penderecki's, *String Quartet* (1960); George Rochberg's, *Time–Span* (II) (1962); and Iannis Xenakis' *Achorripsis* (1957).

Hutcheson, Robert Joseph, Jr.: "Twentieth century Passion settings: An analytical study of Max Baumann's Passion', Op. 63; Frank Martin's 'Golgotha'; Krzysztof Penderecki's 'St. Luke Passion'; and Ernst Pepping's 'Passionsbericht des Matthäus'," PhD dissertation, Washington University, St. Louis, Missouri, 1976, 133 pages, musical examples

This dissertation sets out to investigate four selected musical settings of the New Testament Passion story composed in the twentieth century. Technical analysis of the music, various traditions of biblical criticism, an awareness of the dynamics of faith, and interviews with most of the composers of the works studied aided in the investigation. The centrality of the cross in Christianity is asserted at the outset, and the character of God as One who "suffers" is discussed in relation to the idea of kenosis. To set the scene for each composer's setting of the Passion story, the human tendency to feel that God hides himself or that He is near to man is discussed. This is done to highlight man's response or lack of response to challenges to Christian witness arising out of modern anti–Christian policies and events. The works chosen for study are: Ernst Pepping's *Passionsbericht des Matthäus* (1950); Krzysztof Penderecki's *St. Luke Passion* (1966); Max Baumann's *Passion,* Op. 63 (1959); and Frank Martin's *Golgotha* (1948). The closing chapter discusses the motivating reasons for a composer's choosing to set the Passion story to music and the problems such a decision engenders.

Albers, Bradley Gene: "De natura sonoris I and II by Krzysztof Penderecki: A comparative analysis," DMA dissertation, University of Illinois, Urbana–Champaign, Illinois, 1978, 116 pages

Polish music in the twentieth century from Szymanowski to Penderecki is the focus of this study. It characterizes the cultural milieu into which Penderecki was born and out of which his music eventually grew. The study also traces the evolution and appearances of some of the composer's works on the international scene, drawing attention to a few corresponding experiments with sonic articulation and actualization. A comparative discussion of *De natura sonoris I* and *II* with regard to instrumentation, essential linguistic devices, construction of vertical sonorities, serial structures, rhythmic structures, formal structures and performance realization follows.

Roberts, Gwyneth Margaret: "Procedures for analysis of sound masses," Ph.D dissertation, music theory, Indiana University, Bloomington, Indiana, 1978, 237 pages, musical examples, bibliography

A theoretical study that describes the emergence of the sound mass as a compositional technique as found in the cluster works of Henry Cowell, the complex polyphony of Alban Berg and Charles Ives, and the coloristic effects produced by use of static textures in the works of Olivier Messiaen and Edgar Varèse. The study presents a basic approach to analysis of sound–mass compositions through a detailed study of György Legeti's *Atmospheres*; Iannis Xenakis's *Pithoprakta*; Krzysztof Penderecki's *De natura sonoris*; and Witold Lutosławski's *Trois poèmes d'Henri Michaux*. The sound masses found in these works include sustained clusters, multi–voiced canons, foreground–background effects, and aleatoric devices. These are examined in terms of the component elements, the individual lines, the relationships between the lines, and form and structure.

Bersano, James Richard: "Formalized aspect analysis of sound texture," Ph.D dissertation, music theory, Indiana University, Bloomington, Indiana, 1979, 340 pages, musical examples, bibliography

A method of analysis is developed in this study by which certain aspects of sound texture can be organized in a systematic manner. The central thesis of the method employed is that each aspect of sound texture can be measured on the same intensity scale throughout a composition and that the interpretation of the resultant intensity curves will yield significant information about the style and structure of the composition. The aspects selected for study are activity, density, loudness, register and timbre. George Crumb's *Echoes of Time and the River* (last movement), György Legeti's *Cello Concerto*, Olivier Messiaen's *Chronochromie*, and Krzysztof Penderecki's *Fluorescences* are analyzed according to the method. A system of computer programs is used in the construction and interpretation of intensity tables. Results confirm the usefulness of the method and suggest that it may be extended to other aspects of music besides sound texture.

Brooks, Richard James: "Structural functions of 'Musical Gesture' as heard in selected instrumental compositions of the twentieth century: a graphic analytical structure." Ph.D, NewYork University, New York, 1981, 463 pages, musical examples

The aim of this study is to develop a graphic analytical method which can be applied to selected twentieth century instrumental compositions in order to determine the presence and structural function of musical gesture, which is defined in the study as "a sound subjected to at least one parametrical alteration." It accounts for the notion of sonic motion and therefore bears kinesthetic and affective components which are essential to it but which are not the direct concern of this paper. Eight works are selected for analysis according to five compositional categories: extended tonality (Milhaud's "Midi" from *Une Journée* and Della Joio's *Duo Concertato*), non–metrical atonality (Schoenberg's *Sechs kleine Klavierstücke*, Op. 19, no. 4), serial atonality (Webern's *Saxophone Quartet*, Op. 22 and Babbitt's, *Composition for Four Instruments*), aleatoric (Morgan's *Four Visions*, Op. 2), sound–structure compositions (Penderecki's *Anáklasis* and Ussachevsky's *A Piece for Tape Recorder*). All of the works analyzed reveal the presence of gestural structure and activities.

Daley, Paul Byron: "An investigation of textural activity and its hierarchial structures in selected works by Krzysztof Penderecki." MA, North Texas State University, Denton, Texas, 1984, 111 pages, musical examples, notation

This study is a masters degree thesis that focuses on temporal aspects of the music of Krzysztof Penderecki as they relate to textural activity. The analyses presented are based on a referential idea called a discrete sound event, defined as "an occurrence of a sound or collections of sounds which, as a unit, is distinct from the surrounding texture." These sound events are then used to appraise textural activity from layer fluctuation and composite density. The pieces selected in the application of these techniques are *Threnody* (1960), *Fluorescences*, (1962) and the *Capriccio for Oboe and Strings* (1965).

Delisi, Daniel Joseph: "Compositional techniques and use of the chorus in five selected choral works of Krzysztof Penderecki," DMA document, choral conducting, University of Cincinnati, Ohio, 1985, 129 pages, musical examples, bibliography, list of works, charts, tables

Penderecki's choral works represent a large portion of his compositional output and illustrate many of his important innovations in vocal and instrumental writing. The primary characteristics of his early and middle period works (1956–74) are an exploration of vertical textures and sonorities, and experimentation with and utilization of new kinds of vocal and instrumental tone production. The composer's more recent works utilize a more lyric and less dissonant style. These developments and changes in his style are illustrated in the five works examined in this study: *Stabat mater* (1962), *Dies irae* (1967), *Ecloga VIII* (1972), *Te Deum* (1980), and *Lacrimosa* (1981). All show a balance between innovation and the use of traditional musical elements, in particular a careful control of form.

Murdock, Katherine Ann: "The 'Pittsburgh Overture' by Krzysztof Penderecki" Ph.D, University of Rochester, New York, 1986, 207 pages, musical examples

The *Pittsburgh Overture* (1967) by Krzysztof Penderecki marked a significant addition to the literature of the contemporary wind ensemble. Therefore an analysis of the work provides an important insight into the composer's compositional style and process in writing for wind instruments. The unusual instrumentation and orchestrational techniques of the *Overture* are examined as they contribute to the creation of textural blocks of sound. Set–class analysis is employed to illuminate Penderecki's free approach to the twelve–tone method in his organization of pitch materials, and a discussion of formal construction emphasizes the importance of the wedge shape on several structural levels. While the *Pittsburgh Overture* does not exhibit a consistent application of the twelve–tone technique and the formal organization does not conform to any traditional or symmetrical structure, the study suggests that the work is powerful and effective, largely due to Penderecki's intuitive sense of dramatic pacing and gesture.

Colwell, David Bruce: "Questions of content and context in Krzysztof Penderecki's 'Magnificat'—Including an analysis of the relationship between text and music," MA thesis, Yale University. New Haven, Connecticut, 1985, 154 pages, musical examples

The first American study on the composer's *Magnificat* was completed at Yale University in 1985 by a Canadian master's degree student. The focus of this study is Penderecki's use of the text in one of his most experimental and technical works for chorus and orchestra. The author asks the question: "Can a musician gain insight into a piece of music by considering other elements [How does the piece communicate?] as well as the concrete materials of the music?" By examining the context in which Penderecki has been living and composing works such as *Magnificat*, as well as by exploring the content of the music, the author strives to show that the consideration of elements other than musical ones is not only important but essential to the full understanding of this work.

Bylander, Cynthia E.: "The Warsaw Autumn International Festival of Contemporary Music, 1956–1961: Its Goals, Structures, Programs, and People." Ph.D, The Ohio State University, 1989, 552 pages, tables, list of works, appendix, discography, bibliography

The Warsaw Autumn Festival was an invaluable component of cultural life in Poland between 1956 and 1961. The program of each Festival was influenced to a large degree by extra–musical considerations that limited the actions of the Festival's organizers: the Polish Composers Union and Poland's Ministry of Culture and Art. Nevertheless, the Festival was acclaimed in many countries for its unique ability to present the prevailing styles of music from Europe, the Soviet Union, and the United States, the latest works by Polish composers, and pieces considered to be the classics of the twentieth century. The historic breakthrough accomplished by the first Festival in 1956 signaled the end of the era of socialist realism in Polish music. Furthermore, the shift in compositional styles apparent in the output of many Polish composers between 1956 and 1961 and the international fame accorded to Bacewicz, Lutosławski, and Penderecki must be attributed to a great degree to the existence of the Warsaw Autumn Festival.

Mandrell, Nelson Eugene, Jr.: "Compositional aspects of two early works for string orchestra by Krzysztof Penderecki." DMA document, University of Illinois, Urbana, Illinois, 1989, 174 pages, musical examples

This study examines two compositions for string orchestra from Penderecki's early career. The primary goal is to codify techniques and procedures which create internal consistencies within *Threnody to the Victims of Hiroshima* and *Polymorphia*. The composer's notion is found to be consistent and highly refined. Many elements of the notation are discussed individually. The organization of the Table of Symbols which precedes each score reflects a scalar organization of pitch and timbre that is exploited throughout the compositions. Each piece has a tripartite structure. Both compositions demonstrate the use proportions in their overall formal planning and in the construction of subsections. The middle sections of *Threnody* is a self–contained structure making use of canon and palindrome, and provides an opportunity to examine the composer's organization of textures, duration, dynamics, articulation, pitches and extended playing techniques. An appendix notes inconsistencies and suggests corrections for what appear to be engraving errors in the published version of *Threnody*.

Emilsson, Gudmundur: "Krzysztof Penderecki's 'Dies Irae' (Auchwitz Oratorio): Aspects of music and literature", DMA dissertation, conducting, Indiana University, Bloomington, 1993, 300 pages, musical examples, bibliography.

A pitch–class analysis of Penderecki's 'Dies Irae' (1967) reveals that the work is not based on a rigid precompsitional scheme. The structure freely mirrors the profound historical, literary, religious and philosophical connotations of the libretto, which is a mosaic drawn from the writings of King David,

Aeschylus, John the Evangelist, Paul the Apostle, Paul Valéry, Louis Aragon, Władysław Broniewski and Tadeusz Różewicz.

Foy, Randolph: "Textural transformations: The instrumental music of Krzysztof Penderecki, 1960–73." DMA dissertation, Peabody Institute of the Johns Hopkins University, 1994, 368 pages, musical examples

Krzysztof Penderecki's works through 1973 have variously been described as *Farbenmusik* (color–music), timbre music, sound–mass compositions, and cluster pieces. Commentators have referred to them as being outside the sphere of music and even impossible to analyse, although they have also received critical acclaim and audience support. The focus of this study is the nature of Penderecki's instrumental works from 1960–73—music in which neither pitch nor rhythmic pulse predominate over other elements. A working definition of a musical texture is developed to facilitate analysis and discussion, then a typology of basic textures in Penderecki's works is explored. A context for the musical analyses is established through the discussion of the European avant–garde of the 1960's, other composers of texture–based music of the time, and Penderecki's own background and early compositional interests. Procedures for the application of a type of textural motivic analysis are explored in an extensive sample analysis of the *Capriccio for Violin and Orchestra* (1967). These analytical techniques are then applied to thirteen other representative instrumental works of Penderecki in texture style, including *Threnody to the Victims of Hiroshima* (1960), *De natura sonoris I* (1967), *Partita* (1972) and the *Symphony No. 1* (1973).

Janzen, Wes: "Performing Krzysztof Penderecki's 'Passio et mors Domini nostri Jesu Christi secundum Lucam': A conductor's preparation" DMA dissertation, University of Cincinnati, Ohio, 1994, 217 pages

The stated purpose of this thesis is to assist conductors who are preparing a performance of Penderecki's *St. Luke Passion.* The study is based on research the author undertook with the cooperation of the composer and included examining the sketches of the work, choral manuscripts, autograph full score, set of orchestral parts, and personal conducting score. Errata, performance–practice questions, tempi, revisions to the score, metric solutions to aleatoric passages, pronunciations, and conducting solutions are among the issues visited in the course of the investigation. The dissertation also documents the entire process of preparing for two performances of the work at the 1990 Oregon Bach Festival. Questions which arose in preparing the work are answered by the composer, who has read the completed study and authorized its publication.

Notes

1. In contrast to scholarly practices on the European continent, graduate music study in the American university has developed around two separate philosophies: the German model leading to the Ph.D, and the uniquely American performance–oriented degree with the nomenclatures D.M.A. (Doctor of Musical Arts), D.M. (Doctor of Music, an earned degree), D.M.E (Doctor of Music Education), etc. The history of master's degres is similar. Consequently the nomenclature for these degrees will vary from university to university.

Contributors

REGINA CHŁOPICKA is Senior Lecturer at the Academy of Music in Cracow, Poland, where she teaches theory and musicology. She is a member of the research team at *Centre Nationale de la Recherche Scientifique* (Paris), a member of the editorial board of *Revue européene bilingue* "Theater–Opera–Ballet" published in Paris (Klinksieck), and a member of the *Societé Francaise d'Analyse Musicale.* Professor Chłopicka's main areas of academic research are contemporary Polish music — Krzysztof Penderecki and Witold Lutosławski; the theme of death in music—the requiem and passion genres from Gregorian chant to the 20th century; and problems of modern methods of the analysis of music. She has written more than 50 articles on 20th Century music.

IRINA NIKOLSKA is a Russian musicologist who holds the title of Professor at the Institute of Art, Academy of Science in Moscow. Her primary research interest is 20th century music. She has written extensively on Polish contemporary music, including numerous articles and books. Her published works include *From Szymanowski to Lutosławski and Penderecki* (1990), *Conversations with Witold Lutosławski* (1994) and *Conversations with Krzysztof Penderecki* [in press].

MARIA PIOTROWSKA is a Professor at the Academy of Music in Warsaw. Her graduate studies were concentrated on the problems of aesthetics in the field of 20th century music with particular interest in the area of music and hermeneutics. Professor Piotrowska is also the author of two books: *Neoklasycyzm w muzyce XX wieku* [Neo–classicism in 20th century music] (Warsaw, 1982) and *Tezy o możliwosci hermeneutyki muzycznej w świetle stu lat jej historii* ["Theses about the possibilities of the hermeneutics of music in light of the 100 year history of music"] (Warsaw, 1990).

RAY ROBINSON is Distinguished Professor of Choral Studies at Palm Beach Atlantic College in West Palm Beach, Florida. He is the author *of Choral Music: A Norton Historical Anthology* (W.W. Norton, 1978), co–editor of *A Bach Tribute* (Bärenreiter Verlag, 1994), and a contributor of more than fifty articles that have appeared in a variety of journals, including the *Choral Journal, Essex Institute Historical Collections, Journal of Research in Music Education* and *Schütz Jahrbuch.* With Allen Winold he is the co–author of *A Study of the Penderecki 'St. Luke Passion'.* His university teaching appointments have included Indiana University School of Music, Peabody Conservatory of Music, Westminster Choir College, Wolfson College (Cambridge University), and Palm Beach Atlantic College.

WOLFRAM SCHWINGER retired in 1991 as Opera Director at the State Theater in Stuttgart, Germany, where he initiated the first Penderecki Festival, the 1979 Stuttgart Penderecki Days, which opened with the German premiere of *Paradise Lost*, followed by The *Devils of Loudun*, the ballet *Galileo's Dream* (to Penderecki's First Symphony), the German premiere of the *Violin Concerto No. 1*, as well as chamber and vocal works. Dr. Schwinger, who has been a music critic in Berlin, Hannover and Stuttgart, is the author of *Penderecki: Begegnungen, Lebensdaten, Werkkommentare* (Stuttgart, 1979; London, 1989; Mainz, 1994). His early contacts with Penderecki date from 1964.

ROBERT SHANKOVICH is Professor of Music at Duquesne University in Pittsburgh, Pennsylvania, where he specializes in courses dealing with music analysis and the history and philosophy of music theory. He is the Director of Graduate Studies in the School of Music as well as the founding editor of the journal, *Music theory: Explorations and Applications.*

MAREK STACHOWSKI is a Polish composer, teacher and music administrator. He studied composition and music theory under Krzysztof Penderecki at the Academy of Music in Cracow. He has won awards at many composers' competitions including the musical award of the town of Monchengladbach (1976), the Award of the City of Cracow (1979), the awards of the Minister of Culture and Fine Arts (1981, 1989, for his works for children) and the Jurzykowski Foundation Prize in New York. Besides composing he teaches at the Academy of Music. Until 1979 he also taught at the Jagellonian University. He has taught at Yale University (1978), lectured at summer courses in Durham (England), and led seminars during the Gaudeamus Music Week in Holland (1979, 1984), and at the Rubin Academy of Music and Dance in Jerusalem (1987). Since 1993 he has been Rector at the Academy of Music in Cracow.

MIECZYSŁAW TOMASZEWSKI is a Polish musicologist and Professor at the Academy of Music in Cracow, where he heads the Faculty of Music Theory and Interpretation. For many years he served as Director of the Music Publishing House, Polskie Wadawnictwo Muzyczne (PWM). He has written extensively on the ontology of musical works, problems of the Word–Tone relationship in music, and Polish music of the 19th and 20th centuries. He is author of the following books: *Polish Composers and Chopin* (1959), *Pisma muzyczne O. Kolberga* (1981), *Chopin. A Diary of Images* (1990), *Krzysztof Penderecki and his Music: Four Essays* (1994) and the multi–media publication *Chopin. Życie twórcy* (1995, CD–ROM). He is also the editor of *The Chopin Library* and co–editor of *Chopin Studies* and *Res Facta.*

ALLEN WINOLD is Professor Emeritus at Indiana University School of Music where he taught music theory and music literature for 37 years. He is also a former faculty member of the *Hochschule für Musik* in Vienna, Austria. The author of 12 books and numerous articles, Professor Winold has specialized in music analysis and computer applications in music. With Ray Robinson he wrote *A Study of the Penderecki 'St Luke Passion'*". He is also active as a violist and chamber musician.

MISSION STATEMENT

The purpose of "Studies in Penderecki" is to identify, disseminate and encourage scholarly research on the life and work of the Polish composer, Krzysztof Penderecki. Activities in support of this purpose include meetings, discussions and symposia. The purpose is achieved (1) through the publication of new studies, the republication of outstanding articles and the commissioning of new research topics on the composer and his time; and (2) through the distribution of this information on a world–wide basis through print, computer networks and other media channels of communication.

GUIDELINES FOR PUBLICATIONS

The following outline of general guidelines for these studies was adopted by the Editorial Board at its meeting on June 23, 1994 in Cracow, Poland. Certain elements were considered essential for the purpose of dealing with the topic in its broadest possible context.

1. General perspectives
   a. Synthesis of all aspects of the composer's career
   b. Monographic and general views on the phenomenon of Penderecki
   c. Problems of outstanding and particular importance

2. Penderecki within the context of his time
   a. Penderecki and contemporary currents in music and culture
   b. Penderecki and Polish music
   c. Penderecki and his contemporaries

3. New works
   a. Facts about the newest works
   b. Conversations with the composer about his latest works
   c. Interpretations of his works from various points of view
   d. The texts of vocal works
   e. Photographs from first performances

4. Analysis and interpretation
   a. Old and new works in general as well as detailed interpretations
   b. Discussions of works by categories:
      (1) Stage works
      (2) Oratorios, Masses, Cantatas, etc.

        (3) Symphonic works
        (4) Concertos
        (5) Choral works
        (6) Chamber music
        (7) Solo works

5. Aspects of Penderecki's music
   a. Early avant–garde style
   b. Notational innovations
   c. The composer's use of the orchestra (voices)
   d. Neo–romantic elements in Penderecki's music
   e. Stylistic synthesis in the later works
   f. New directions in his music

6. Archives: Reprints of older articles that are still valid today and contain historical interest

7. The composer speaking about himself, his music and his world
   a. Interviews
   b. Speeches
   c. Discussions
   d. Responses at award ceremonies

8. Penderecki's life and activities
   a. Personal history
      (1) Childhood
      (2) Formative years
      (3) Teaching career
      (4) Conducting career
      (5) Travels
      (6) Hobbies
   b. Periods of creativity (style periods)

9. Documentation—Sources of information about his life, works, and activities compiled chronologically and by subject
   a. Chronology
   b. Works
   c. First performances
   d. Conducting documentation (works, highlights, etc.)
   e. Prizes, decorations, honorary doctorates, awards

10. Reception (*Rezeptions Geschichte*)
    a. Studies concerning how Penderecki's works have been received in various countries and cultures
    b. The phenomenon of the popularity of his music

11. Bibliography
    a. Annotated listing of articles similar to the RILM system
    b. Retrospective according to subjects

12. Discography—Annotated listing of recordings

13. Biographical information about the authors

LIST OF WORKS

1953* *Sonata* for violin and piano

1955 *Cisza* ("Silence") for solo voice and piano (Words by Leopold Staff, from *Wiklina*, 1954) [unpublished]

1955 *Niebo w nocy* ("Sky at night") for solo voice and piano (Words by Leopold Staff, from *Wiklina*, 1954) [unpublished]

1956 *Miniatures* for clarinet and piano

1957 *Oddech nocy* ("The Breath of Night") for voice and piano (Words by Leopold Staff, from *Dzięwieć muz*, 1958) [unpublished]

1957 *Prośba o wyspy szczęśliwe* ("A Plea for the Happy Isles") for solo voice and piano (Words by K. Ildefons Gałczyński, 1930) [unpublished]

1958 "Epitaphium Artur Malawski in memoriam" for string orchestra and timpani [unpublished]

1958 *Psalms of David* for mixed choir, strings, and percussion

1958 *Emanations* for two string orchestras

1959 *Strophes* for soprano, speaking voice, and 10 instruments

1959 *Miniatures* for violin and piano

1960 *Anáklasis* for string orchestra and percussion

1960 *Dimensions of Time and Silence* for mixed choir, strings, and percussion

1960 *Threnody to the Victims of Hiroshima* for 52 strings

1960* *String Quartet No. 1*

1961 *Fonogrammi* for flute and chamber orchestra

1961 *Psalmus 1961* for tape [unpublished]

1961 *Polymorphia* for 48 strings

1962 *Canon* for string orchestra and tape

1962 *Fluorescences* for symphony orchestra

1962 *Stabat Mater* for 3 mixed choirs a cappella (Later used in the *St. Luke Passion*)

1963 *The Death Brigade* for tape (Radio drama) [unpublished]

1964 *Cantata in honorem Almae Matris Universitatis Iagellonicae sescentos abhinc annos fundatae* for mixed choir and orchestra

1964 *Sonata* for violoncello and orchestra

1965 *Capriccio* for oboe and 11 strings

1966 *Passio et mors Domini nostri Jesu Christi secundum Lucam* for solo voices, speaking voice, boys choir, mixed choir, and symphony orchestra (Composed 1962-1966)

1966 *De natura sonoris No. 1* for symphony orchestra

1967 *Dies irae—oratorium ob memoriam in perniciei castris in Oświęcim necatorum in exstinguibilem reddendam* for solo voices, mixed choir, and symphony orchestra

1967* *Pittsburgh Overture* for wind orchestra, timpani

1967 *Capriccio* for violin and orchestra

1968 *Capriccio for Siegfried Palm* for solo violoncello

1968 *String Quartet No. 2*

1969 *The Devils of Loudun*—Opera in 3 acts (Libretto by the composer based on Aldous Huxley and the stage play by John Whiting

1970 *Utrenja I*—The Entombment of Christ for solo voices, 2 mixed choirs, and symphony orchestra (Composed 1969-70)

1970* *De natura sonoris No. 2* for symphony orchestra

1970* *Cosmogony* for solo voices, mixed choir, and symphony orchestra

1971 *Utrenja II*—The Resurrection of Christ for solo voices, 2 mixed choirs, and symphony orchestra (Composed 1970-71)

1971 *Prelude* for wind orchestra

1971 *Actions* for jazz ensemble

1972* *Partita* for harpsichord, electric guitar, harp, doublebass and orchestra (Revised 1991)

1972 *Concerto No. 1* for violoncello and orchestra (Composed 1967-1972; revised version of the "Concerto for Violono Grande")

1972 *Ecloga VIII* for 6 male voices

1972 *Ekecheiría* for tape (Composed for the opening ceremony of the Olympic Games in Munich, Germany) [unpublished]

1973 *Canticum canticorum Salomonis* for 16-voice mixed choir and orchestra

1973 *Symphony No. 1* for symphony orchestra

1973 *Intermezzo* for 24 strings

1974 *Magnificat* for bass solo, 7-part male vocal ensemble, 2 mixed choirs, boys' choir, and orchestra

1974 *The Awakening of Jacob* for symphony orchestra

1976 *Concerto No. 1* for violin and orchestra

1978* *Paradise Lost—sacra rappresentazione* in 2 acts (Libretto by Christopher Fry based on John Milton)

1979 *Adagietto* from *Paradise Lost* for orchestra

1979 *Prelude, Visions, and Finale* from the opera *Paradise Lost* for large chorus and orchestra

1980* *Symphony No. 2* for symphony orchestra

1980 *Capriccio* for tuba solo

1980 *Te Deum* for solo voices, choir, and orchestra

1980 *Lacrimosa* for soprano, choir, and symphony orchestra (Later incorporated into the *Polish Requiem*)

1981 *Agnus Dei* for a cappella choir (Later incorporated into the *Polish Requiem*)

1981 *Czyś ty snem była* ("Were you but a dream"), song for baritone and piano (Words by K. Przerwa-Tetmajer, from *Poezje, seria druga*, 1894) [unpublished]

1982 *Concerto No. 2* for violoncello and orchestra

1983 *Concerto for Viola and Orchestra* (formerly called "Elegie for Viola and Orchestra")

1984 *Cadenza* for viola solo (violin version by Christiane Edinger)

1984 *Polish Requiem* for solo voices, choir, and symphony orchestra (Composed 1980 to 1984, "Sanctus" movement added in 1993)

1986 *Die schwarze Maske* ("The Black Mask"), opera in one act, libretto by the composer and Henry Kupfer, based on Gerhardt Hauptmann

1986 *Per Slava* for violoncello solo

1986* *Cherubim Song* for a cappella choir

1987 *Prelude* for clarinet solo

1987 *Veni Creator* for a cappella choir

1988 *Der unterbrochene Gedanke* for string quartet

1988 *Passacaglia and Rondo* for symphony orchestra (Incorporated into *Symphony No. 3* in 1995)

1989 *Adagio* for symphony orchestra (*Symphony No. 4*)

1990 *Ubu Rex* ("King Ubu"), opera buffa, libretto by Jerzy Jarocki and Krzysztof Penderecki based on the play "Ubu Roi" of Alfred Jarry

1991 *String Trio* for violin, viola, and violoncello (Composed 1990-91)

1991 *Sinfonietta* for string orchestra [This work is a revision of the *String Trio* (1991)]

1992 *Benedicamus Domino* for a cappella men's chorus

1992 *Symphony No. 5* ("Korean") for orchestra (Composed 1991-92)

1992 *Concerto for Flute and Chamber Orchestra*

1993 *Quartet for Clarinet and String Trio*

1995 *Divertimento* for unaccompanied cello

1995* *Entrata* for brass instruments

1995 *Agnus Dei* for the *Requiem of Reconciliation*

1995 *Symphony No. 3 for Orchestra* (including the movements *Passacaglia and Rondo*)

1996 *Symphony No.* 7 ("The Seven Gates of Jerusalem") for solo voices, choir, and symphony orchestra

1997 *Hymne an den heiligen Daniel* ("Hymn to the holy Daniel") for choir and winds

1997 *Hymne an den heiligen Adalbert* ("Hymn to the holy Adalbert") for choir and winds

1998* *Credo* for soloists, choir and symphony orchestra

* American premieres